BLESS THIS
TABLE

Celebrity Family Recipes

By Teri Diamond
& Jaymes Foster

Published by Blessed Productions, First Edition 2013

Copyright © 2012 by Teri Diamond & Jaymes Foster

ISBN: 978-0-9896226-0-8

Design: Dawn Rodgers Wyse

Cover and Food Photography: Steve Diamond

Food Preparation and Styling: Teri Diamond

Back Cover Photo and Authors' Photos: Dominick Guillemot

Printed by TSE Worldwide Press Inc. in China.

www.BlessThisTable.com   TXu 1-812-861 July 2012

Special Thanks

A very special thanks to the celebrities:

Alison Krauss, Andrea Bocelli, Cat Cora, Celine Dion, Clay Aiken, Dave Koz, David Foster, Donna Summer, Josh Groban, Melissa Manchester, Michael Bublé, Natalie Grant, Orianthi, Quincy Jones, Reba, Richard Marx, Rita Wilson, The Cox Family, The Pointer Sisters, Vince Gill & Amy Grant, Wolfgang Puck and Wynonna.

Additional thanks:

Steve Diamond, Cole Diamond, Dawn Rodgers Wyse, Louise Krauss, Veronica Berti, Marc Johnston, Allessia Narvarino, Rene Angelil, Dave Platel, Paul Farberman, Mark Johnson, Faye Parker, Catherine Aiken, Roberta Wilson, Ruth Copley, Jeannie Copley, Maureen Martyn, Marylou Eales, Bruce Sudano, Lindy and Jack Groban, Gayle Fine, Sharon Vaughn, Amber and Lewis Bublé, Mitch and Yolanda Santaga, Mitchel Solarek, Adam Fell, Narvel Blackstock, Cliff Williamson, Cynthia Marx, Jay Landers, Christie Cox, Jean Ann McNally, Deanna Hemby, Alison Auerbach, Yolanda Hadid Foster, Maggie Boone, Kerry Hansen, Jennifer Witherell, Connie Bradley, Barry Landis, Dominick Guillemot, Judith Guillemot, Danelle Rondberg, Sarah Tse, Polly Keith, Susan Pomerantz, Farrell Mason, Holly Bell, Sylvia Brown, Pam Mathis, Gretchen Mathis and Marc Mathis.

From the Authors

My fondest childhood memories were the weeks spent at my grandmother, Mama Todd's home in Jackson, Tennessee. Many of these memories were centered around her kitchen table. I was amazed at how many cousins she could fit around that table. I can still remember the smell of her fried chicken and fresh vegetables that were prepared from her garden. Her desserts were always home made and as I inherited her "dessert gene," I truly appreciated the fact that she always served at least two desserts at our gatherings. Rolls and biscuits that would melt in your mouth were served with her unforgettable pear preserves. She was not the type to tell you often that she loved you. Her showing of affection was through her gift of cooking. And what a gift it was! We were never allowed to eat until she said Grace and that instilled in me the importance of appreciating the bountiful food that was prepared with love for us. I now carry on the tradition of my grandmother by preparing special meals for my family where we share quality time together. This is what inspired me to create Bless This Table with Jaymes. We thought it would add to the treasure of preparing family meals to have the special recipes of celebrities that we admire. It's a special part of their life that they are sharing with us. As they continue to make memories with these dishes that they prepare for their families, we are given the opportunity to do the same.

—Teri Diamond

One thing for sure in our Foster household was that everyday around the same time we would all sit down together and have dinner at the table. That experience stayed in my soul and now as an adult, I still believe that it's important to gather all at the dinner table and share the events of the day and what happens to be on your mind. Today, in our hurried lives, this tradition seems to be going by the wayside for various reasons. My hope is that this book of memories of family dining experiences may inspire families to sit together and enjoy each other over a great meal.

—Jaymes Foster

Introduction

The focus of this book is the importance of family dinners and what a nurturing tradition it is to prepare a special meal for those you love. Sharing food and conversation around the dining table with your family creates magical memories that will help you grow as a family and stay in your hearts forever. It is an important tradition that you can hand down from generation to generation.

This book contains treasured family recipes from celebrities' personal lives that have special meaning to them. They have been generous to share these delicious meals with us which they prepare for their own families. Many of the recipes have been passed down from previous generations.

Bless This Table is a celebration of family meals throughout the world. From Michael Bublé's grandmother's Italian feast to Celine Dion's mother in-law's Middle Eastern treats to Wolfgang Puck's Austrian delights from his mother. Of course, it contains many wonderful dishes from regions of the U.S. including the Pointer Sister's chicken and dumplin's recipe from their mother to Amy Grant's mother's cherished chicken salad recipe.

Enjoy these special family recipes and memoirs shared by these celebrities. Here's to wonderful family gatherings in the years to come!

Table of Contents

Alison Krauss

Alison is a celebrated American bluegrass-country singer, fiddler and record producer. She has been awarded 27 Grammys for her extraordinary talent, making her the most decorated female recording artist in Grammy history.

 FAMILY MEAL

KONIGSBERGER KLOPSE (GERMAN MEATBALLS)

PARSLEY POTATOES

GREEN BEANS WITH PEARS AND BACON

My grandmother, Martha Malchow Krauss, made Konigsberger Klopse (which are German meatballs) at some of our family gatherings. I was told she got the recipe from my great grandmother. Growing up, this was one of my favorite dishes and I'm happy to share it with Bless This Table. The parsley potatoes and green beans with pears recipe, that I have included, really go well with this dish.

KONIGSBERGER KLOPSE
(GERMAN MEATBALLS)

INGREDIENTS

1 pound ground pork

1 pound ground beef

1/3 cup bread crumbs

2 onions
(1 grated and 1 finely chopped)

Salt, pepper and nutmeg to taste

5 egg whites, stiffly beaten

3 cups water

4 bay leaves

1 tablespoon sugar

1 teaspoon salt, for sauce

1/4 cup tarragon vinegar, or to taste
(should be tart)

1/2 teaspoon allspice and
peppercorns, combined

1 tablespoon flour or cornstarch

5 egg yolks, beaten

1 lemon, sliced

Capers

Sour cream, optional

DIRECTIONS

Mix meat, grated onion, bread crumbs, salt, pepper and nutmeg.

Add stiffly beaten egg whites.

Shape into balls about the size of a walnut. Set aside.

For the sauce, boil water, finely chopped onion, bay leaves, sugar, 1 teaspoon salt, allspice and peppercorns mixture for 30 minutes.

Strain sauce. Bring back to boiling point.

Add meat balls and simmer for about 15 minutes, repeating the process until all meatballs are cooked.

Remove all meatballs from pan and place on a serving dish. Add vinegar to remaining liquid in pan.

Dissolve flour in small amount of cold water. Add beaten egg yolks.

Gradually add to seasoned liquid, stirring constantly until smooth and thick.

Pour over meatballs. Garnish with lemon slices, capers and sour cream if you choose. Serve with extra sauce.

PARSLEY POTATOES

INGREDIENTS

2 pounds small new potatoes

1 stick butter, melted

1 tablespoon fresh parsley,
finely chopped

Salt to taste

DIRECTIONS

Wash potatoes well and keep skins on. Cut potatoes in half.

Put potatoes in large pan. Cover with water.

Add salt to pan. Cook on medium heat.

When potatoes start to boil, lower heat but continue to boil 15 to 20 minutes or until tender. Drain water from potatoes.

Salt to taste.

Pour melted butter over potatoes.

Sprinkle in parsley.

Gently fold mixture to coat potatoes well.

GREEN BEANS WITH PEARS AND BACON

INGREDIENTS

1 pound green beans, trimmed

4 slices bacon

4 ripe pears, peeled and sliced

1 cup water

1 teaspoon salt

¼ cup sugar

1 teaspoon fresh lemon juice

2 tablespoons white vinegar

DIRECTIONS

Snap beans into broken pieces.

In medium size pan, add pear slices with water.

Cook on medium high heat.

When water begins to boil, lower heat and simmer until pears are cooked. This will only take about 5 minutes.

Add green beans and salt. Continue cooking on low heat.

Fry bacon in skillet until crisp. Drain bacon and crumble. Set aside.

Discard all but 2 tablespoons of the bacon fat from skillet.

Add vinegar, lemon juice and sugar to skillet and stir with a whisk on low heat until smooth and well blended.

Pour sauce into pan with green beans and pears and continue cooking until beans are tender.

Transfer green beans to bowl and add crumbled bacon.

Alison's Blessing

Thank you for the people gathered here today at our table.

Please bless this food and thank you for the love given to prepare it.

In Jesus' name,

Amen.

Andrea Bocelli

Andrea is an operatic tenor with a voice of rare beauty. He has graced the stages around the world from New York's *Carnegie Hall* to *The Rome Opera*. Andrea has sold over 75 million CDs worldwide and has been awarded many honors, including recently a star on *Hollywood's Walk of Fame*.

 FAMILY MEAL

FILLET OF VEAL
WITH MUSHROOMS

SPAGHETTI WITH OLIVE OIL
AND GRATED TRUFFLE

FROZEN YOGURT

ESPRESSO COFFEE

I think dining together at the table is one of the most important moments for the family, because it's a reunion: parents and children speak freely, they exchange thoughts and ideas… it's a moment that improves the relationship between them. For example, I try to teach my sons what my dad taught me when I was a child. I ask what they did at school…I give them suggestions and advice, that slides down between a dish and another. Eating with family might also be a good way to learn to eat properly: children learn to eat vegetables and fruits for example and they acquire an "imprinting" that will last for all their life… habits difficult to change forward in time.

Andrea Bocelli

FILLET OF VEAL WITH MUSHROOMS

INGREDIENTS

Fillet of veal, 4 pieces

5 Porcini mushrooms, finely chopped or mushroom of choice*

5 teaspoons cream

2 tablespoons butter

2 teaspoons brandy

1 large clove garlic, thinly sliced

1 teaspoon fresh parsley, chopped

Salt and pepper, to taste

DIRECTIONS

Add butter to large sauté pan.

Cook at medium heat until butter has melted.

Add veal to pan and cook on both sides.

As veal is cooking, add garlic and mushrooms.

Once mushrooms are cooked, pour the brandy over the veal.

Add the cream.

When sauce is creamy, remove from heat and sprinkle with parsley, salt and pepper.

Transfer to serving dish.

*You can char grill the mushrooms before adding to dish for extra flavor if you prefer.

SPAGHETTI WITH OLIVE OIL AND GRATED TRUFFLE

INGREDIENTS

1 pound spaghetti

3 tablespoons extra virgin olive oil

White truffle, to taste

¼ teaspoon salt

DIRECTIONS

In large pot, heat 6 quarts of water and add salt.

When water begins to boil, add the spaghetti and cook for 10 minutes.

Drain the spaghetti and put in large bowl.

Gently stir in olive oil to coat the spaghetti.

Grate the white truffle on pasta as you would parmesan cheese.

Serve immediately.

FINISH WITH FROZEN YOGURT ESPRESSO COFFEE

Cat Cora

Cat Cora is the co-host of Bravo's *Around the World in 80 Plates* and the only female Iron Chef on Food Network's *Iron Chef America*. In addition, Cat is the author of 3 top-selling cookbooks and a children's book, a restaurateur, and contributing food and lifestyle editor for *O*, the Oprah Magazine, making her one of the most recognized names in the culinary community. Cat designs her own line of versatile cookware and gourmet *Cat Cora's Kitchen* food products, as well as her own collection of wines. Outside of the kitchen, Cat is an avid philanthropist and in 2004 she founded *Chefs for Humanity*, which is dedicated to eradicating hunger and obesity with an emphasis on a holistic global sustainable approach.

FAMILY MEAL

KOTA KAPAMA
(GREEK CINNAMON STEWED CHICKEN)

MAKARONIA
(BUTTER AND CHEESE NOODLES)

CAT'S CARAMELIZED BRUSSELS SPROUTS

HORIATIKI
(TOMATO, CUCUMBER, FETA
AND GARLIC COUNTRY SALAD)

ALMA'S ITALIAN CREAM CAKE

My mom always worked and yet somehow, every birthday, she pulled out all the stops and made exactly what we wanted for dinner. What I wanted, every year, was Kota Kapama. Exceptionally tender and flavorful, it's one of those dishes that sits on the back of the stove all afternoon, filling the house with lush aromas. I liked it so much, I'd bribe my younger brother to ask for it on his birthday too, and it's a dish I love still as much today as I did as a kid.

Photo by Michael Spain-Smith, courtesy Cat Cora

We'd hardly ever have Kota Kapama without rich and savory Makaronia, which are super flavorful butter and cheese noodles. Why serve plain pasta when a little cheese and butter gives noodles so much more pizzazz? Brussels sprouts are underrated, but this version is truly irresistible with brown butter, capers, and Parmesan — my kids love them! I'd bet even the biggest skeptics will never be able to pass them up again. Horiatiki is a classic Greek salad but my favorite non-Greek, my partner Jennifer, taught me to twist this up by topping it with sautéed garlic, caramelized until crispy and sweet, and this is now exactly how I always make it.

You can't end a perfect meal better than with a nice big piece of my Grandma Alma's Italian cream cake. She served this cake for anniversaries, birthdays, funerals, weddings, baptisms -- you name it, and it's the most silky, moist cake, with frosting so luscious and creamy you can't keep your fingers away from it no matter how hard you try!

Two things in my memory never fail to make me happy when I think of them — my Alma, and this cake.

Keep Cooking!

XXOO

Cat Cora

GREEK CINNAMON STEWED CHICKEN
(KOTA KAPAMA)

INGREDIENTS

1 chicken (2 ½ to 3 pounds), cut into 8 pieces

1 teaspoon ground cinnamon

2 teaspoons Kosher salt

1 teaspoon freshly ground black pepper

5 peeled garlic cloves

2 tablespoons extra virgin olive oil

2 peeled, coarsely chopped medium yellow onions

½ cup dry white wine

1 cup water

1 cup chicken stock

1 (6-ounce) can tomato paste

1 tablespoon fresh oregano, chopped

½ cup grated Mizithra cheese

DIRECTIONS

Pre-boil water with sea salt.

Pat the chicken dry with paper towels. A wet chicken will cause the oil to splatter while the chicken is sautéing. Mix the cinnamon, salt and pepper in a small bowl. Rub the chicken pieces on all sides with the seasoning.

Mince 3 of the garlic cloves. Heat the olive oil in a large non-reactive deep skillet over high heat. A 12-inch skillet with sides about 2 ½ to 3 inches high will allow you to brown all the chicken at once. If you don't have a skillet large enough, brown them in two batches using ½ the oil for each batch. What's important is that the chicken isn't overcrowded which would cause them to steam rather than brown.

Add the chicken to the oil and brown for about 4 to 5 minutes on each side. Turn the pieces using a metal spatula, as they have a tendency to stick to the pan. Remove the pieces when well browned on all sides.

Lower the heat to medium-high and add the onions and minced garlic. Cook for about 3 minutes, stirring constantly, until the onions have softened and are a rich golden brown. Add the wine and scrape the bottom of the pan with a spatula or spoon to deglaze the pan, loosening any particles stuck on the bottom.

When the wine has evaporated, add the water, chicken stock, tomato paste, fresh oregano and remaining 2 garlic cloves. Return the chicken to the pan. The liquid should cover about ¾ of the chicken pieces. Cover the pot and simmer over low heat for about an hour or until the chicken is tender and thoroughly cooked. If the sauce becomes too thick, it can be thinned with a little more water. Season the finished sauce with kosher salt and pepper to taste.

Serve the chicken topped with the sauce and sprinkle with Mizithra cheese.

BUTTER AND CHEESE NOODLES
(MAKARONIA)

INGREDIENTS

1 tablespoon kosher salt, plus 1 ½ teaspoons

10 ounces egg noodles, elbow macaroni, penne, or rigatoni

3 tablespoons unsalted butter

3 tablespoons grated sheep's cheese (kasseri or pecorino) plus ½ cup for serving

¼ teaspoon freshly ground black pepper

DIRECTIONS

In a large saucepan, bring 4 quarts of water to a boil.

Add 1 tablespoon of the salt and the pasta and cook until al dente, 5 to 7 minutes. Drain well.

In a large sauté pan, melt the butter over medium-high heat.

Add the drained pasta and the 3 tablespoons grated cheese.

Season with the remaining salt and pepper and toss well.

Top with the remaining cheese and serve hot.

CAT'S BRUSSELS SPROUTS

INGREDIENTS

3 pounds Brussels sprouts

1 tablespoon plus 1 teaspoon kosher salt

4 tablespoons unsalted butter

¼ cup capers, drained

2 tablespoons fresh lemon juice

½ teaspoon freshly ground black pepper

2 tablespoons grated Parmesan cheese, for garnish

DIRECTIONS

Prepare the Brussels sprouts by peeling off the tired outside leaves and cutting off the stem. Mark the core where the stem was with an X using a paring knife. Cut the sprouts in half.

In a 4 quart sauce pan bring 2 quarts of water to a boil. Season with 1 tablespoon of salt. Blanch the sprouts for 10 minutes, or until fork tender.

In a 10-inch sauté pan, brown the butter and add in the sprouts. Cook on medium high heat, rolling the sprouts in the pan, until the sprouts are well caramelized on all sides, about 10 minutes.

Remove from the heat, and add the capers, lemon juice, pepper and remainder 1 teaspoon of salt. Sprinkle with cheese.

TOMATO, CUCUMBER, FETA AND GARLIC COUNTRY SALAD (HORIATIKI)

INGREDIENTS

4 minced, large garlic cloves

1 tablespoon plus 1 cup extra virgin olive oil

3 large ripe tomatoes

1 large cucumber

1 small red onion

12 Kalamata olives

1 cup crumbled Feta cheese

½ cup red wine vinegar

1 tablespoon chopped, fresh oregano

Kosher salt

Freshly ground black pepper

DIRECTIONS

In a small sauté pan, sauté the garlic in 1 tablespoon of the olive oil over medium-high heat, stirring often, until the garlic is caramelized and slightly crunchy.

Remove the core from the tomatoes and slice each tomato into ¼ inch slices. Peel the cucumber and slice into ⅛ inch slices. Peel the onion and slice into thin rings. Arrange the vegetables on individual plates or a platter. Sprinkle the olives and cheese over the vegetables.

Mix together the vinegar, olive oil and oregano. Season each salad with salt and pepper, drizzle with the dressing, and the reserved garlic and oil.

ALMA'S ITALIAN CREAM CAKE

INGREDIENTS FOR CAKE

2 cups cake flour

1 teaspoon baking soda

½ teaspoon salt

12 tablespoons (1 ½ sticks) unsalted butter, softened to room temperature

2 cups granulated sugar

5 large eggs, yolks & whites separated, at room temperature

1 cup buttermilk

1 teaspoon vanilla extract

1 cup sweetened shredded coconut (angel flake)

1 cup finely chopped walnuts, toasted

INGREDIENTS FOR CREAM CHEESE FROSTING

1 cup chopped walnuts, toasted

1 8-ounce package cream cheese, softened

8 tablespoons (1 stick) unsalted butter, softened

1 tablespoon vanilla extract

4 cups (1 pound) confectioners' sugar, sifted

DIRECTIONS FOR THE CAKES

Place a rack in the middle of the oven and preheat oven to 350°F.

Prepare 2 round 9-inch cake pans by greasing and flouring them or by cutting a circle of parchment to fit each pan, greasing the pan, fitting the parchment into place, and then greasing the parchment.

Sift the flour, baking soda, and salt into a medium bowl and set aside. In the bowl of a stand or with a hand mixer, cream the butter and 1 ½ cups of the sugar until light and fluffy. Add egg yolks one at a time beating well after each addition. Add the sifted dry ingredients and buttermilk in thirds to the creamed mixture, beating on medium speed after each addition and wiping the sides of the bowl down with a rubber spatula. Add vanilla, coconut and nuts and mix well.

In a separate bowl, whip the egg whites with cleaned beaters, slowly adding the remaining ½ cup of sugar and beating until the whites form stiff peaks but are not dry. Carefully, fold one third of the egg white mixture into the batter until all is incorporated. Fold in the next third of the egg whites and when that's incorporated, gently fold in the last third.

Divide the batter evenly into the 2 prepared pans.

Bake until the top is golden brown and a wooden toothpick comes out clean when inserted in the middle of the cake, about 30 to 35 minutes.

Let the cakes cool completely before removing them from the pans.

DIRECTIONS FOR THE CREAM CHEESE FROSTING

Beat the cream cheese, butter and vanilla at medium speed with an electric mixer until creamy.

Add powdered sugar, one cup at a time, beating at low speed until blended. When all the ingredients are incorporated, beat the frosting at high speed until smooth. Stir in ½ cup of the toasted walnuts.

Ice the sides and top of one cake before placing the other cake on top. Place the frosted cake in the refrigerator to firm up the frosting.

Remove the cake from the refrigerator about 30 minutes before serving, and press the remaining ½ cup of walnuts into the frosting on top.

DIRECTIONS TO TOAST THE WALNUTS

Toast the chopped walnuts in a shallow baking pan at 325°F for about 5 to 7 minutes or until the nuts are fragrant. Remove the pan from the oven and let the nuts cool.

Celine Dion

Celine Dion has won just about every award that a singer can receive, including the World Music Award for being the best-selling female artist of all time. While she appreciates the recognition associated with her many accomplishments, her greatest joy comes from being a mother.

FAMILY MEAL

STUFFED VINE LEAVES

FRIED CAULIFLOWER

MEAT TARTS (SFIHAS)

I'm very happy to be able to share these recipes with everyone. They were a gift to me from Rene's late mother, Alice Angelil.

Alice was such a warm and gentle person who adored her children and she loved family get-togethers with everyone gathered around the dinner table sharing great food and great conversation. I always looked forward to when Alice would be doing the cooking because I knew I was going to be in for some delicious treats. Of course, Rene was in heaven every time he had the chance to savour his mom's home-cooking!

Even when we vacationed together, Alice would find her way to the kitchen to whip up some goodies for all of us. It was so great for me, because I was introduced to Middle-Eastern food "home-style" ...and it doesn't get better than this! Since Alice left us, we've continued the tradition of our favorite dishes and Rene and I are able to pass on this wonderful tradition to our children. For "Bless This Table," I've included three of my favorites, which go together to create a wonderful meal.

I sincerely hope that you will enjoy these tasty delights as much as we do and I wish all of you many, many wonderful family times together.

With love,

Celine Dion

STUFFED VINE LEAVES

STUFFING INGREDIENTS

50 vine leaves, usually sold in jars

½ cup of long-grain rice

¼ cup of olive oil

1 medium sized onion, finely chopped

½ pound of ground lamb

¼ cup of parsley, finely chopped

2 tablespoons of fresh mint, finely chopped

3 large spoons of fresh lemon juice

½ teaspoon of turmeric

½ teaspoon of dried oregano

1 egg

Salt, to taste

Special Arabian pepper (finely milled white and black pepper, cardamom, nutmeg, 4 spices, cloves and cinnamon ... blend portions of each spice to your personal taste)

INGREDIENTS FOR COOKING

1 teaspoon of finely chopped garlic

2 teaspoons of olive oil

2 tablespoons of fresh lemon juice

¼ cup of water

DIRECTIONS

Put vine leaves in a large bowl and submerge them in boiling water. Let stand for 20 minutes, then rinse and drain well.

Separate the leaves and place them on a clean white towel. Set aside any broken leaves; you'll use these for lining the bottom of the cooking pot (see later).

Boil rice for 5 minutes, and drain away any excess water. Using a non-stick frying pan, sauté the onion in oil for about 10 minutes. Add lamb and cook well.

Turn off heat, then add the rice and all of the other stuffing ingredients... mix everything together very well. This is your final stuffing.

Spread out 30 vine leaves on a platter or clean surface and cut off the ends of each leaf. Put one tablespoon of the stuffing on each leaf and roll carefully tucking the sides so that the stuffing will be secured in each leaf. You now have 30 little stuffed leaf "packages."

Cover the bottom of a big pot with 10 vine leaves (you can use any ones that may have broken, or complete leaves). Place the 30 "packages" in the pot, with the open seam facing the bottom of the pot. Add the oil, garlic, lemon juice and water. Cover the "packages" with the remaining 10 vine leaves and place a plate on top to secure everything. Quickly bring to a boil, then reduce heat and simmer (covered) for about 50 minutes. Uncover and let-stand for a while so that you'll be serving the dish at room temperature. Tahini sauce is an excellent condiment, if so desired!

FRIED CAULIFLOWER

INGREDIENTS

2 large cauliflowers

Oil for frying

Salt, to taste

Arabian pepper (see vine leaves)

DIRECTIONS

Blanch the cauliflower in a pot for about 10 minutes in salted water.

Remove from pot, break the cauliflower into flowerets and pat dry on a paper towel.

Heat oil in frying pan to 375 degrees or medium high.

Fry cauliflower for a few minutes then remove and pat dry again.

Season with Arabian pepper (to taste).

MEAT TARTS
(SFIHAS)

INGREDIENTS

1 container of refrigerated crescent dinner rolls

1 pound of ground veal

1 medium sized onion, finely chopped

¼ cup of plain yogurt

2 tablespoons pine nuts, roasted

1 egg

Salt, to taste

Arabian pepper (see vine leaves)

DIRECTIONS

Remove crescent roll dough from container and divide each triangle strip in half.

From each half triangle, shape dough into 3" diameter circular tarts and flatten the edges... leave the center thicker.

Mix all of the stuffing ingredients with your hands and spread this mixture on the tarts (sfihas) to within ¼ inch of the edges.

Place sfihas on a greased cookie sheet and bake at 375 degrees for 7 to 10 minutes on the lower rack.

Move to the upper rack and bake for an additional 5 minutes.

Clay Aiken

Clay's singing career began on the hugely successful television show *American Idol*. He has sold millions of CDs, launched 8 tours, authored a New York Times best-selling book and made his Broadway debut in Monty Python's *Spamalot*. In addition to being a UNICEF Ambassador, he created the National Inclusion Project, which encourages and facilitates community inclusion of individuals with disabilities.

 FAMILY MEAL

GLAZED HAM

GRANNY AND FAYE'S
HOT PINEAPPLE SALAD

BABY LIMA BEANS

CREAMED POTATOES

BUTTERMILK BISCUITS

PEACH PIE

Few can argue that the smells of the kitchens of our childhood can bring back memories decades old.

My grandmother never took a cooking class. Like so many women of her generation, Catherine Clayton Aiken learned to cook out of necessity. She had no cookbooks to guide her and no television cooking show hosts to cheer her along. All she had was a hungry brood at the table.

So, she made meal after meal for her family of five for years in the same green kitchen in Bahama, NC. And when those children grew up and had their own children, she cooked for them too in that same small, green kitchen, forming some incredible memories for all.

We all know the smell of her scratch made biscuits, the ones she makes and places in the yellow tin pot, with the lid on tight to keep them warm.

Whether it was her home-made biscuits or her glazed hams at Christmas, no one has ever made food taste quite like Granny has. The smells that came from that tiny farm house kitchen could entice a family -- now grown to twenty-nine, including great grandchildren -- to huddle around a small kitchen table to enjoy a meal crafted by the most talented, self taught hands to ever grace a stove.

She's in her mid eighties now. Papa has passed and she now lives alone. The kitchen has even been remodeled for her. And, whether she's got company coming over or not, she still has something cooking on that stove everyday. And, one rarely leaves her home without a special treat she's prepared for you to take with you.

Clay

GLAZED HAM

INGREDIENTS

Ham, fully cooked (10 to 12 lbs)

2 tablespoons light brown sugar

1 tablespoon of plain bread crumbs

3 tablespoons honey

1 teaspoon ground cloves

DIRECTIONS

Preheat oven to 375 degrees.

Combine brown sugar, bread crumbs and cloves in small bowl. Rub mixture over entire ham.

Place the ham in a shallow roasting pan and bake for 15 minutes or until the sugar dissolves.

Remove from oven and drizzle honey on the ham.

Return to oven and cook for 15 to 20 minutes more.

GRANNY AND FAYE'S HOT PINEAPPLE SALAD

INGREDIENTS

1 large can pineapple chunks

1 cup sugar

6 tablespoons self rising flour

2 cups sharp cheddar cheese, grated

1 stick of butter

1 sleeve of butter crackers

DIRECTIONS

Put first 4 ingredients in a 2 quart baking dish and mix.

Crush crackers and layer on top.

Melt stick of butter and pour over mixture.

Bake at 350 degrees for 30 minutes.

BABY LIMA BEANS

INGREDIENTS

Family size package of baby lima beans

¾ stick of margarine or butter

½ teaspoon sugar

½ teaspoon minced onion or
2 teaspoons of dried minced onion

DIRECTIONS

Put lima beans in a large stock pot.

Cover with water.

Add margarine or butter, onions, salt, pepper and sugar.

Cook until beans are tender.

CREAMED POTATOES

INGREDIENTS

6 to 8 medium sized potatoes, peeled and cubed

½ stick of margarine or butter

½ cup milk

Salt and pepper, to taste

2 tablespoons sour cream, optional

½ teaspoon of garlic salt, optional

DIRECTIONS

Place potatoes in large pot and cover with water.

When potatoes begin to boil, turn down heat slightly and let them continue to boil until potatoes are soft when pierced with a fork.

Drain and pour into large mixing bowl.

Add margarine or butter, salt, pepper and milk.

With mixer, stir until smooth.

Add sour cream or garlic salt if you choose.

BUTTERMILK BISCUITS

INGREDIENTS

2 cups all purpose flour, sifted

2 ½ teaspoons baking powder

½ teaspoon salt

½ teaspoon baking soda

¼ cup shortening

¾ cup buttermilk

DIRECTIONS

Preheat oven to 450 degrees.

Sift dry ingredients into large bowl.

Cut in the shortening with a fork or pastry cutter.

Add the buttermilk and blend until the dough holds together.

Turn out on a floured board. Knead a few times and roll out to ½ inch thickness.

Flour round biscuit cutter and cut biscuits 2 inches in diameter.

Place on a slightly buttered cookie sheet.

Bake for 12 to 15 minutes or until lightly browned.

PEACH PIE

INGREDIENTS

2 to 3 cups fresh peaches, peeled and sliced

¾ to 1 cup sugar, depending on taste

½ stick of butter or margarine, softened

2 tablespoons flour

2 pie crusts

DIRECTIONS

Preheat oven to 350 degrees.

Put peaches in large mixing bowl.

Add sugar, butter or margarine and flour.

Mix well.

Pour into one pie crust.

Top with the second pie crust.

With a fork, prick a few holes in top crust.

Bake for 30 to 40 minutes, allowing the top to brown.

Clay's Blessing

Our Father,

We thank you for the blessings in our life.

We thank you for each other and the rest of our family.

Guide and direct our paths and forgive us of our trespasses.

Bless this food to the nourishment of our bodies

and our bodies to Your service.

Amen.

Dave Koz

Grammy-nominated saxophonist Dave Koz has recorded a dozen albums which spawned multiple Top 5 hits and have landed on the top of the Contemporary Jazz album charts. In addition to touring worldwide, he hosts his *Dave Koz Radio Show* that is syndicated internationally on the airwaves.

Dave has served for 17 years as global ambassador for the Starlight Children's Foundation. In 2006 Starlight honored Dave with the Humanitarian Of The Year Award. In addition, Dave received a star on the Hollywood Walk of Fame.

FAMILY MEAL

AUDREY'S FAMOUS CHEESE KNISHES

CHEESE KUGEL

BRISKET

THE FAMOUS AUDREY KOZ HOMEMADE CHOCOLATE CHIP COOKIES

Photo by Greg Allen, courtesy Dave Koz

I grew up in a Jewish household with a stereotypical Jewish mother…her name was Audrey Koz. Of course, we ALL feel this way about our moms…but she was the greatest! Of course, now that she's been gone for many years, I would give ANYTHING for one last meal of hers. Cooking was the way she showed love…preparing her signature dishes for those she cared about most. Well, Audrey made a LOT of people happy in her lifetime with her dishes, let me tell you…she was always in the kitchen!

We had a very lively dinner table growing up—it was very important for my mom to have the whole family sit down every night together, to eat and discuss the day. It was the BEST…I miss those days so much. Thankfully, my sister Roberta has taken up the mantle and kept Audrey's famous "Jewish Soul Food" recipes alive, bringing them into a new generation. After traveling to far-flung locales, it's always my first request…to go over to Roberta's house and humbly ask her to cook some 'mom food' for me…to have an old-fashioned Koz Family dinner. Happily, she never says no! Nothing comforts like these recipes. And in this way, they live on forever…spreading my mom's unique brand of love to the world. I am thrilled to be able to include a dose of "Audrey Love" here in Bless This Table with you. She would have loved it! Enjoy!

AUDREY'S FAMOUS CHEESE KNISHES

INGREDIENTS

4 packages of hoop cheese or farmer's cheese (approx. total 2 pounds)

2 egg yolks

¼ cup sugar

Salt and pepper, to taste

Frozen puff pastry sheets

DIRECTIONS

Defrost puff pastry sheets.

Mix cheese together with egg yolks, sugar, salt and pepper.

When soft, cut pastry sheets down the middle width wise. Roll with rolling pin so that pastry sheet is very thin (crepe like). Pastry sheet should be longer horizontally than vertically.

Place cheese mixture along the bottom of the pastry sheet horizontally (about 1 inch thick right along the bottom edge of the sheet.) Roll up the pastry sheet around the cheese and continue rolling all the way to the top so you have a "log".

Starting at the far right edge, tuck in the loose pastry sheet into the log. Using the side of your hand, cut about a 2 inch piece and then tuck the other end of the knish back into the center.

Flatten the knish to a round shape which is about 1 inch high. Repeat for the whole log and it should make 6 knishes. Repeat for all pastry sheets in the box. One box of puff pastry sheets should make about 24 knishes.

Bake in oven at 400 degrees until nice and golden brown, approximately 30 minutes.

CHEESE KUGEL

INGREDIENTS

3 packages farmer's cheese

1 package hoop cheese

2 bags egg noodles (cooked)

½ pint sour cream

7 eggs, beaten

1 teaspoon salt, or more to taste

1 tablespoon sugar

DIRECTIONS

Spray a 13 x 9 pan (glass works great).

Mix all ingredients together in a large bowl.

Pour into prepared pan.

Bake at 375 degrees for 45 to 60 minutes (should be golden and a bit crispy on top).

BRISKET

INGREDIENTS

1 (5-ounce) bottle garlic sauce

1 (10.5-ounce) can beef broth

1 (12-ounce) can tomato paste

Salt and pepper, to taste

Garlic powder, to taste

1 brisket, about 4 lbs

DIRECTIONS

Mix garlic sauce, beef broth, and tomato paste together in a bowl.

Sear the brisket on both sides with salt, pepper and garlic powder.

Place brisket in roasting pan and pour the sauce all over it.

Bake at 350 degrees for 3 to 3 ½ hours.

Slice brisket when cool. For even more tender meat, put sliced brisket back in the oven for another hour before serving.

THE FAMOUS AUDREY KOZ HOMEMADE CHOCOLATE CHIP COOKIES

INGREDIENTS

¹/3 cup butter, softened

¼ cup canola oil

½ cup white sugar

½ cup brown sugar

1 large egg

½ teaspoon vanilla

1 ½ tablespoon hazelnut liqueur

1 ½ cups flour

½ teaspoon baking soda

1 ½ cups chocolate chips

1 English toffee bar chopped into small pieces

½ to 1 cup whole pecans or ½ cup walnuts

DIRECTIONS

Cream butter, oil, sugar and egg until creamy.

Add vanilla and liqueur.

Add baking soda to flour and add to the sugar mixture.

Add chocolate chips, nuts and toffee bar pieces.

Drop by generous tablespoons on ungreased cookie sheet about 2" apart.

Bake at 350 degrees for 15 to 17 minutes or until golden brown.

Cool and remove from sheet.

Makes about 25 to 30 cookies.

David Foster

A Golden Globe recipient and sixteen-time Grammy Award winning record producer, songwriter and artist, Canadian David Foster has worked with superstars Celine Dion, Barbra Streisand, Mary J Blige and Andrea Bocelli, to name a few. As a music executive with his own 143 record label, he has developed the careers of Michael Bublé, Josh Groban and The Corrs. His David Foster Foundation is dedicated to providing financial support to Canadian families with children in need of life-saving organ transplants.

 FAMILY MEAL

ROAST BEEF WITH VEGETABLES

GRAVY

YORKSHIRE PUDDING

NANAIMO BARS

Can you imagine growing up in a household with 6 sisters and no brothers!?? Actually it was pretty great. But then can you imagine our mother, Eleanor, having to cook for 9 people putting meals on the table 3 times a day?? And, with no help and a small budget to do so. Not only did she do that but she also made her own bread! I value the time our family spent around the dining room table. We were the generation of being home for dinner at the same time every day. We never ate in restaurants except on one of our birthdays, as a special treat. Our house was the house that everyone gravitated to ...which also meant that we, at many times, had many more people eating meals at our table. The more the merrier. And, every Sunday night was the same special dinner... roast beef with Yorkshire pudding and all that goes with that. So, those are the dishes I wanted to share in Bless This Table. Along with my favorite, Nanaimo Bar for dessert...a famous Canadian treat named after the town on Vancouver Island, the Island where we all grew up.

Looking back... whenever anyone asks me about my childhood, all I can ever say is that in my mind it was perfect. This, I believe, has given me a great advantage in my own life, career and family time. There is nothing more precious than family to me and although as children we took our mealtimes at the dinner table for granted, that tradition stayed with me for my lifetime and is part of my roots. By sharing my favorite meal with all of you, it also means that I'm happily sharing a very personal part of me with you.

David Foster

ROAST BEEF WITH VEGETABLES

INGREDIENTS

One 5 to 10 pound roast (butt is most tender and flavorful cut)

8 cloves of garlic

1 stick butter

Salt and pepper, to taste

1 pound of baby carrots

5 large russet potatoes, peeled and cut in large wedges

INGREDIENTS FOR GRAVY

4 tablespoons flour

1½ to 2 cups beef broth

Salt and pepper, to taste

DIRECTIONS

Preheat oven to 425 degrees. Season beef with salt and pepper. With a very sharp knife, make a few slices all around and top of the roast. Insert whole cloves of garlic into slits. Rub butter over the roast.

Put beef in lightly buttered roasting pan. Add baby carrots and potatoes around the roast. Roast meat for 30 minutes.

Reduce the heat to 325 degrees and continue to roast, allowing 12 minutes per pound for rare (meat thermometer, 120 to 125 degrees), or 14 to 15 minutes per pound for medium (meat thermometer, 140 degrees).

Allow it to stand 15 minutes before slicing.

GRAVY

Spoon off all but 4 tablespoons of fat from roasting pan. Whisk flour into fat until the flour is cooked fully and is no longer white. Slowly add beef broth. Season with salt and pepper. Continue to stir with a whisk over low heat until gravy thickens.

YORKSHIRE PUDDING

INGREDIENTS

1 cup whole milk

3 eggs

1 cup sifted flour

¼ teaspoon salt

1 tablespoon cold water

Hot drippings from roast beef

DIRECTIONS

Mix eggs and milk. Add flour and salt. Let batter rest on the counter at room temperature for 30 minutes to 2 hours. Add 1 tablespoon cold water to the batter just before baking.

Fill each of the 12 muffin tins with 1 teaspoon of hot drippings from the roast. Pour batter in the muffin tins, filling them about one-third full. The batter will sizzle in the hot drippings.

Bake at 400 degrees for 30 to 40 minutes until the puddings are puffed and browned. Just before removing puddings from the oven, prick each one with a fork — this lets the steam escape so they can crisp in the oven.

NANAIMO BARS

BOTTOM LAYER INGREDIENTS

½ cup butter

2 to 4 tablespoons sugar

5 tablespoons cocoa

1 egg, beaten

2 cups graham cracker crumbs

¼ to ½ cup coconut,
unsweetened finely chopped

¼ cup walnuts or pecans,
finely chopped (optional)

SECOND LAYER INGREDIENTS

¼ cup butter

3 tablespoons half & half
or whole milk

2 tablespoons vanilla custard powder

2 cups powdered sugar
(icing sugar), sifted

THIRD LAYER INGREDIENTS

4 squares semisweet chocolate
baking squares

2 tablespoons butter

DIRECTIONS

Bottom Layer: Melt first 3 ingredients in top of double boiler or in heavy saucepan.

Add beaten egg and stir to cook and thicken.

Remove from heat.

Stir in crumbs, coconut and nuts (if using). Press firmly into an ungreased 9 x 9 pan. CHILL.

Second Layer: Cream butter, custard powder and half & half together then add sifted powdered sugar, mixing well. Beat until light.

Spread over bottom layer. CHILL.

Third Layer: Melt chocolate squares and butter over low heat. COOL.

When cool but still runny, spread over second layer. CHILL.

Use sharp knife to cut into squares before completely set.

Donna Summer

Grammy award winner, singer songwriter Donna Summer earned an astonishing 14 top 10 hits culminating in record album sales of 130 million copies. Donna is the first female artist to have three #1 solo singles in one year and was the first artist to have three consecutive double albums reach #1 on the US Billboard chart. In addition to her recording and performing career, Donna was an accomplished visual artist whose work has been shown at exhibitions worldwide. Along the way, Donna lent her talent in support of *UNICEF* and many other charitable causes. In 2013 Donna was postumously inducted into the Rock and Roll Hall of Fame.

FAMILY MEAL

HIGH OCTANE SALAD
(For People on the Go)

What do you get when you put together an Italian-American boy from Brooklyn, an African-American girl from Boston, and the house Meryl Streep lived in, in the film "It's Complicated"... you get "LA DOLCE VITA". If home is where the heart is, then the table surrounded by its inhabitants is the heartbeat and food the fuel that keeps that heart beating.

So the first thing we did upon purchasing our home was to put in an enormous organic garden. I did lots of cooking, baking and entertaining. I knew great food, shared experiences, laughter and a little tomfoolery would be foundational in cementing a lifetime of precious memories. For me the dinner table is Grand Central, where we all get together, take stock, unload the day and appreciate who we really are. Our family would sit, hold hands and begin by singing grace...and this is what we'd sing...

Thank you God, Thank you God
For our food today
Oh the Lord is good to me
And so I thank the Lord
For giving me the things I need
The sun, the rain and the apple tree
The Lord is good to me
For every seed I sow
I know a tree will grow
And there will be an apple tree
For everyone in the world to see
The Lord is good to me
Amen amen amen AMEN   —Donna

HIGH OCTANE SALAD (For People on the Go)

INGREDIENTS FOR DRESSING

3 fresh lemons

Cold pressed virgin olive oil

Celtic salt or sea salt & black pepper

INGREDIENTS FOR SALAD

Avocado

Kale (approx. 2 leaves, cut away the stem)

Baby spinach (approx. 1 handful)

Endive (1 endive medium size sliced in rings)

Baby romaine (1 head per person, shredded 1/2 inch thick) If not available use regular romaine lettuce

Butter lettuce (approx. 8 leaves)

Red radish (4 to 5 medium size, thinly sliced)

Radicchio (½ large, shredded)

Red & yellow pepper (1 small or ½ large chopped)

Baby cucumber (2 sliced)

Red onion (small sliced)

Fresh mint (3 stalks finely chopped)

Fresh basil (3 stalks finely chopped)

Fresh cilantro (1 inch thick bunch, finely chopped)

OPTIONAL: Hearts of palm, green olives, toasted sliced almonds

DIRECTIONS

I suggest you buy your fresh produce from the organic section of your local supermarket. After washing and preparing the fresh vegetables, toss all the ingredients except the avocado into one large bowl.

Slice lemons in half, remove the seeds and squeeze the juice of the lemons directly over the salad. Toss and begin to add the sea salt.

After all the lemon juice is evenly distributed throughout the salad, sprinkle the extra virgin olive oil over the salad and toss again, all the while adding salt and pepper to taste. The sea salt will bring out flavors that regular salt will not bring out.

Just before serving, slice avocado from top to bottom in half, open and remove seed. Take a large spoon and scoop the avocado from its skin. Turn facedown and slice from top to bottom 5 times and then slice it into squares and toss into salad.

You are now finished with the salad…at this point you may feel free to begin singing "I work hard for the money"!

Be creative add your own beloved herbs… If there is something that you particularly like, then add it! There are no salad police!

Enjoy!

Josh Groban

Grammy-nominated singer songwriter Josh Groban has sold an amazing 25 million CDs and DVDs and has entertained fans touring around the globe. In addition, Josh is an accomplished actor and has performed in the feature film *Crazy, Stupid, Love* as well as appeared on many TV shows including *The Office, The Simpsons, Ally McBeal* and *Glee*.

Josh has performed at many events supporting charities and in July, 2011 he founded his *Find Your Light Foundation,* which is dedicated to enriching the lives of young people through quality arts education.

 FAMILY MEAL

GROBAN FAMILY BRUNCH EGGS
(Our Christmas Morning Tradition!)

My dad and brother and I were very lucky that my mom likes to cook. She's always loved to whip up new things but there were certain classics that we literally salivated for all year long. This egg dish is something of a legend in our family. Sure, presents are fun. But I wouldn't totally be lying if I said we opened quickly to get to the good stuff. I hope your family enjoys this dish as much as we have.

BRUNCH EGGS
(Our Christmas Morning Tradition!)

INGREDIENTS

1 can whole kernel corn

2 tablespoons butter

1 dozen eggs

1 ½ cups sour cream

½ cup milk

4 cups shredded cheddar cheese

1 (4-ounce) can diced green chiles

1 tablespoon Worcestershire™ sauce

1 tablespoon salt

1 teaspoon pepper

DIRECTIONS

Drain the corn and lightly sauté in butter, put aside.

Combine all the other ingredients, add the corn.

Grease a 9 x 13 pan.

Bake at 325 degrees for 1 hr. 15 min.

You can easily substiute salt free canned corn, low fat milk, sour cream and cheese if desired. Can also be prepared one day ahead.

Serve with salsa, guacamole, chips or cornbread.

Melissa Manchester

Grammy Award winning artist, songwriter, and film composer Melissa Manchester is the first recording artist in the history of the Academy Awards to have two nominated movie themes in a given year. Additionally, Melissa is an acclaimed actor and has starred in the national tours of Andrew Lloyd Weber's *Music of the Night* and *Song and Dance* and she also created the role of Maddy on the NBC television hit series *Blossom*. Melissa is the recipient of the National Academy of Recording Arts and Science's Governor's Award for her contributions to the music and recording arts. When she's not away on one of her concert tours, Melissa loves to cook delicious food for her family and friends.

 FAMILY MEAL

NO BIG DEAL BIG DEAL CHICKEN

DUTCH OVEN ROASTED POTATOES

LEMON CAKE

Photo by Randee St. Nicholas, courtesy Melissa Manchester

This is a photo of my mother, the fabulous Ruth Manchester, with my sister Claudia, on the right, and me. Mom knew how to live with style, whether in feast or famine. She always made life and food a feast for my dad, sister and me or the twenty-or-so friends or family members that might drop by on a moment's notice. Dining together was charged with good conversation and delicious tastes – mouth and soul memories I'm happy to share with you. When my own family had dinner we would say what we were thankful for each day and we always ended our grace with "Thank you God for your faith in us."

Melissa Manchester

NO BIG DEAL BIG DEAL CHICKEN

INGREDIENTS

2 whole chickens

1 package chicken breasts
(and wings if you wish)

2 small bottles Heinz 57™ sauce

4 onions

4 tomatoes

1 package baby carrots

Salt, pepper, granulated onion,
granulated garlic, turmeric, paprika

DIRECTIONS

Cut up whole chickens and cut chicken breasts in half.

Schmear on 1 bottle of Heinz 57™ sauce.

Season to taste with salt, pepper, granulated garlic, granulated onion, turmeric and paprika.

Put flour in the bottom of a turkey-sized roasting bag.

Cut up onions, tomatoes and baby carrots. (I cook by color, so make sure the colors look balanced – add more tomato, carrot or onion as needed.)

Toss all of the veggies in the bottom of the roasting bag. Cover with the second bottle of Heinz 57™ sauce.

Place the chicken on top of the veggies and close the bag. Make 6 slits in the bag.

Place the bag in a baking pan.

Roast in the oven one hour at 400 degrees and one hour at 350 degrees.

Enjoy!

DUTCH OVEN ROASTED POTATOES

INGREDIENTS

Small red potatoes, 3 or 4 per serving

Garlic powder

Onion powder

Freshly ground black pepper

One stick butter or margarine

DIRECTIONS

Scrub and dry small red potatoes.

Place in a Dutch oven.

Generously sprinkle garlic powder, onion powder and ground black pepper on top.

Place stick of butter or margarine on top of the potatoes.

Cover the Dutch oven and place over a low flame.

After 30 minutes, lift the lid and turn the potatoes as they brown.

Repeat as needed. It takes about 1 ½ hours to finish.

You're gonna like them!

LEMON CAKE

INGREDIENTS

1 (18.25-ounce) box lemon supreme cake mix (with pudding in the mix)

1 cup sour cream

Juice of 1 lemon

½ cup plus 2 tablespoons oil

4 eggs

GLAZE INGREDIENTS

The juice of 1 lemon

1 ½ to 2 cups powdered sugar

DIRECTIONS FOR CAKE

Butter and flour bundt pan.

Mix cake mix, sour cream, lemon juice, oil and eggs and pour into prepared pan.

Bake at 350 degrees for 40 minutes or until wooden toothpick inserted in the center comes out clean.

When cake is cool, invert onto a plate.

DIRECTIONS FOR GLAZE

Mix together the juice of 1 lemon and 1½ to 2 cups powdered sugar in a small bowl.

Pour glaze over the cake so that it drips down the sides.

Michael Bublé

Singer-songwriter Michael Bublé's way around a romantic song has brought him tremendous success with fans and record buyers all over the globe. Michael has sold 45 million CDs worldwide which have earned him 3 Grammy Awards and multiple Junos as well as chart-topping albums and #1 hit singles. Michael continues to support and lend his talent to many charities.

FAMILY MEAL

ANTIPASTO

SALADA

VEGETABLE RISOTTO

CHICKEN DRUMMETTES

PRAWNS

When I'm out touring I can't wait to go back to Vancouver where I was raised and eat a home cooked Italian feast cooked by my mum, sisters and grandmother. The meal I want is what we have been eating for years! We all sit around the dinner table and eat and drink the wine my grandfather makes himself. It's still our whole family's favorite dinner and I'm happy to share it with you!

ANTIPASTO

INGREDIENTS

Sliced melon with thin pieces of prosciutto

Sliced Genoa salami

Thin slices of provolone cheese

Roasted sliced red peppers

Marinated artichoke hearts

Italian bread slices

DIRECTIONS

Arrange on decorative platter each ingredient side by side.

Delicious way to start the meal!

SALADA

INGREDIENTS

1 bag of your favorite types of lettuce

¼ cup red wine vinegar

¾ cup olive oil

Parmesan cheese

Salt & pepper

DIRECTIONS

Slowly whisk olive oil into red wine vinegar.

May want to add more oil or vinegar depending on taste.

Add salt and pepper.

Pour over salad greens and coat leaves.

Sprinkle parmesan cheese on salad and serve.

Simple but delicious!

VEGETABLE RISOTTO

INGREDIENTS

4 tablespoons butter

I onion, chopped

1 yellow bell pepper, chopped

1 large bunch of asparagus, cut into pieces

⅓ cup of mushrooms, sliced

2 to 2¼ cups vegetable stock or chicken stock

1½ cups Arborio (Italian risotto rice)

Salt & pepper

Grated Parmesan cheese

DIRECTIONS

Heat 2 tablespoons of butter in heavy bottom skillet.

Sauté onion and pepper until soft.

Add asparagus and mushrooms. Cook until tender.

Add rice and stir constantly. Gradually pour in veggie or chicken stock.

Keep stirring the whole time while adding stock each time the liquid starts absorbing into the rice.

Do this until rice becomes tender.

Season with salt and pepper.

Before serving add 2 tablespoons of butter and Parmesan cheese to taste.

Serve immediately.

CHICKEN DRUMMETTES

INGREDIENTS

1 large bunch of fresh rosemary, chopped

1 whole head of garlic, chopped

3 tablespoons vegetable oil or more depending on taste

4 tablespoons lemon pepper seasoning salt

3 lbs chicken wings

DIRECTIONS

Preheat oven to 375 degrees.

Add wings to roasting pan.

Mix together rosemary, garlic, lemon pepper seasoning salt and oil. Pour over wings and stir to evenly coat.

Cook for 1 ½ hours.

When one side is good and crispy, carefully turn over with metal tongs or spatula and cook other side until crispy.

Make sure they are cooked well and crisp as this is what makes them taste so good! (Just as good served cold!)

PRAWNS

INGREDIENTS

2 pounds prawns

4 tablespoons vegetable oil

8 cloves of garlic, minced

1 large bunch green onions, chopped

Flour for dredging

Salt and pepper

DIRECTIONS

Butterfly fresh prawns leaving shell only on tail.

Heat oil and sauté garlic for 1 to 2 minutes on high heat. Make sure not to burn garlic.

Add green onions.

Dredge prawns in flour, salt and pepper.

Pan fry with garlic and onions one side at a time until cooked.

Should cook very quickly (1 to 2 minutes per side).

Serve hot and eat instantly!

Delicious!

Natalie Grant

Grammy nominee and five-time Gospel Music Association's Female Vocalist of the Year winner, Natalie is Christian music's top selling female artist. However, her greatest achievements are her twin daughters, Grace and Isabella, and her youngest, Sadie Rose, along with her award-winning producer husband, Bernie Herms. Natalie established *Abolition International* in 2005, a non-profit organization dedicated to educating communities, building shelters, and providing medical equipment to those ministering to the victims of trafficking.

 FAMILY MEAL

MANDARIN SALAD

BAKED HAM WITH MUSTARD GLAZE

CORNFLAKE POTATO CASSEROLE

FRESH GREEN BEANS

BROWNED BUTTER BANANA CREAM PIE

Photo by Dominick Guillemot, courtesy Natalie Grant

I come from a fairly large family. Being the youngest of five children, our days took us all in a hundred different directions. But there was one place where we all connected, one place where busy-ness subsided and togetherness reigned: the dinner table. I am so grateful that my parents never sacrificed that time, and regardless of schedules, never gave in to the temptation to become a "fast food" family.

Some of my fondest memories as a child were formed around the family table. My prayer is that I continue this wonderful tradition with my husband and precious daughters. I want my girls to know what my parents taught me. More than just food, the dinner table is where stories are told, bonds are nurtured, laughter lives, and dreams are discovered.

Though I learned that the dinner table is so much more than food, I also learned a love for great home cooking. Thankfully, my family is full of fabulous cooks. My mom and all of my older sisters are great in the kitchen. Being the youngest, I have inherited some timeless recipes. Baked ham dinner has always been my favorite meal. In fact, my mom would make this for my birthday every year. And when I travel back to Seattle to celebrate, this is still the meal that greets me at the dinner table.

Natalie Grant

MANDARIN SALAD

SALAD INGREDIENTS

¼ cup sliced almonds

1 tablespoon & 1 teaspoon sugar

¼ head iceberg lettuce

¼ head romaine lettuce

2 medium stalks celery, diced

2 green onions, sliced

1 small can mandarin oranges

DRESSING INGREDIENTS

¼ cup vegetable oil

2 tablespoons sugar

2 tablespoons vinegar

1 tablespoon fresh parsley, chopped

½ teaspoon salt

¼ teaspoon pepper

DIRECTIONS

Cook almonds and sugar over low heat stirring constantly until sugar is melted and almonds are coated. Cool and break apart.

Combine all dressing ingredients in a small covered jar and shake to thoroughly combine.

Place lettuce and romaine in plastic bag. Add celery and green onions. Pour dressing in bag and add oranges.

Shake well to mix salad.

Place in a bowl and top with almonds.

Recipe courtesy of my mom, Gloria Grant

BAKED HAM WITH MUSTARD GLAZE

INGREDIENTS

My favorite is a pre-cooked, spiral ham. But whether spiral cut or not, a pre-cooked ham works best and can be purchased at any quality grocer.

GLAZE INGREDIENTS

½ cup pure maple syrup

½ cup brown sugar

½ cup apple juice

1 heaping tablespoon brown or Dijon mustard

Dash cinnamon and ginger or allspice, optional

MUSTARD SAUCE INGREDIENTS

1 cup white sugar

½ cup yellow mustard

¼ cup vinegar (or to taste)

½ cup water

1 tablespoon all-purpose flour

1 egg, beaten

¼ cup butter

DIRECTIONS

Follow instructions on ham package, but general rule for 6 to 8 lb ham: cook at 325° for about 18 minutes per pound, until meat thermometer registers 148°.

Combine glaze ingredients in saucepan; bring to a boil and boil for about 2 minutes (be careful not to let it boil over).

About 20 minutes before the ham is done, spoon about half of the glaze over top of ham, then about 10 minutes before done, spread remaining glaze over ham.

DIRECTIONS FOR MUSTARD SAUCE

Put sugar and flour into a small saucepan. In a separate bowl, mix liquid ingredients.

Combine and cook over low heat until smooth and glossy.

Keep temperature low to avoid curdling the egg.

Recipe courtesy of my mom, Gloria Grant

CORNFLAKE POTATO CASSEROLE

INGREDIENTS

1 (32-ounce) bag hash browns, thawed

1 stick butter, melted

1 tablespoon salt

½ teaspoon pepper

1 (10.75-ounce) can cream of chicken soup

1 (16-ounce) container sour cream

1 (8-ounce) package cheddar cheese

1 medium onion, chopped

TOPPING INGREDIENTS

2 cups cornflakes, crushed

½ stick butter, melted

DIRECTIONS

Mix all ingredients and pour in large 13 x 9 x 2 casserole dish.

Mix cornflakes and butter.

Add as topping to the dish.

Bake for 40 to 60 minutes at 350 degrees.

FRESH GREEN BEANS

INGREDIENTS

2 pounds fresh green beans

4 slices bacon, diced

2 small onions, diced

1 tablespoon oil

2 teaspoons salt

½ teaspoon sugar

¼ teaspoon pepper

DIRECTIONS

Wash and snip off ends of beans.

Snap beans into 1 to 1 ½ inch pieces.

In large skillet, fry bacon and onion until browned.

Add remaining ingredients and stir fry until beans are slightly tender.

BROWNED BUTTER BANANA CREAM PIE

INGREDIENTS

¾ cup white sugar

1/3 cup all purpose flour

¼ teaspoon salt

2 cups milk

3 egg yolks, beaten

2 tablespoons butter

2 teaspoons vanilla extract

1 (9 inch) pie crust, baked

4 bananas, sliced

DIRECTIONS

Cook butter in a small saucepan over medium heat, stirring constantly, 4 to 6 minutes or until butter begins to turn golden brown. Immediately remove pan from heat.

In a 2-quart saucepan, combine the sugar, flour and salt. Add milk in gradually while stirring gently.

Cook over medium heat, stirring constantly, until the mixture is bubbly. Keep stirring and cook for about 2 more minutes, and then remove from the burner.

Stir a small quantity of the hot mixture into the beaten egg yolks, and immediately add egg yolk mixture to the rest of the hot mixture.

Lower heat and cook for 2 more minutes (remember to stir). Remove the mixture from the stove, and add browned butter and vanilla.

Stir until you achieve a smooth consistency.

Slice bananas into the cooled baked pie shell. Top with pudding mixture.

Bake at 350 degrees for 12 to 15 minutes. Chill for an hour.

Recipe courtesy of my sister, Allison Sankey

Natalie's Blessing

Dear Lord,

We recognize that every good thing comes from you.

Thank you for the blessings of this food and our family.

May our conversation around this table

be honoring, loving and encouraging.

It's for Your glory and in Your name we pray, Amen.

Orianthi

Orianthi is an Australian artist and guitarist extraordinare. She is best known for being Michael Jackson's lead guitarist for his *This Is It* movie, and as the lead guitarist in Alice Cooper's live band. Her debut single "According To You" was a huge worldwide hit. In 2009, Orianthi was included on a list of 12 Greatest Female Electric Guitarists by Elle magazine and won the Breakthrough Guitarist of the Year award from Guitar International magazine in 2010.

 FAMILY MEAL

MINESTRONE SOUP

PAVLOVA ROLL
WITH BERRIES AND PASSIONFRUIT

My Mum loves to cook for the family. Whether it is for a birthday celebration or just the family getting together to catch up on what's happening. My Mum, Dad, Grandparents, Auntie and cousins, along with my sister and I gather together for food made with love.

Since I am on the road a lot, and rarely home, the family gatherings have become even more special to me. My Mum's Minestrone Soup and her Pavlova Roll with Berries and Passion Fruit are favorite dishes that I am sharing with you.

Orianthi

MINESTRONE SOUP

INGREDIENTS

1 onion, finely chopped

1 clove garlic, minced

3 medium cans of diced tomatoes or equivalent very ripe, fresh tomatoes

3 potatoes peeled and cubed

3 carrots peeled and sliced

1 cup string beans chopped

1 sweet potato peeled and cubed

1 cup zucchini chopped and /or broccoli

2 cups chicken stock

2 tablespoons of tomato paste

2 cups of ham or veal tortellini

Fresh basil

Shaved Parmesan cheese

Olive oil

DIRECTIONS

Lightly fry onions and garlic in olive oil (Boil for low fat recipe).

Add vegetables (except tomatoes) and fry for 2 minutes.

Add chopped tomatoes, tomato paste, chicken stock, salt and pepper.

Add additional water until large saucepan is nearly full.

Bring to a boil and simmer covered for half an hour.

Add tortellini and chopped basil and simmer for another half hour (or longer for a richer flavor).

Serve topped with Parmesan cheese, additional chopped basil and freshly ground pepper.

PAVLOVA ROLL
WITH BERRIES AND PASSIONFRUIT

INGREDIENTS

¾ cup castor sugar,
(super-fine sugar)
plus extra for sprinkling

6 egg whites

1 teaspoon vinegar

1 teaspoon plain flour

1¼ cups whipping cream

1 teaspoon vanilla extract

1 teaspoon sugar

1 punnet fresh raspberries

1 punnet strawberries

2 passionfruits

Roasted hazelnuts, grated (optional)

Dark chocolate, grated (optional)

DIRECTIONS

Preheat oven to 350 degrees.

Grease a 10" x 12" Swiss roll pan. Line with baking paper, allowing a slight overhang on all sides.

Use an electric mixer to beat egg whites until stiff peaks form. Add ¾ cup castor sugar. Beat for 10 minutes or until sugar has dissolved.

Add flour and vinegar and continue beating for a minute. Spread mixture over prepared pan. Smooth top. Bake for 10 minutes or until top just starts to brown.

Use an electric mixer to whip cream, vanilla extract and sugar until soft peaks form.

Puree ½ cup of mixed berries.

Place a second sheet of baking paper on a flat surface. Sprinkle with the extra castor sugar.

Turn cooked meringue onto prepared baking paper. Carefully remove baking paper. Cool for 10 minutes.

Cover with cream. Top with raspberries and sliced strawberries and passionfruit pulp. Drizzle with berry puree.

Roll up meringue from one long end to enclose filling. Place on a plate and refrigerate for 1 hour. Serve dusted with icing sugar, (or grated roasted hazelnuts or grated dark chocolate).

Quincy Jones

Quincy Jones' career has encompassed the roles of award-winning composer, record producer, artist, film producer, arranger, conductor, instrumentalist, TV producer, record company executive, best selling author, magazine founder and multi-media entrepreneur. As producer and conductor of the historic *We Are The World* recording and Michael Jackson's multi-platinum solo albums, *Off The Wall*, *Bad* and *Thriller* (the best-selling album of all time, with over 65 million copies sold), Quincy Jones stands as one of the most successful and admired creative artist/executives in the entertainment world.

 FAMILY MEAL

CHICKEN, ONIONS, POTATOES AND SAUERKRAUT

GARDEN VEGETABLE SALAD WITH VINAIGRETTE

Most people who are close to me know that there are two things I love more than anything. First would be my family and second the music that I have been associated with. Earlier years, I ate just about everything from ribs to fried chicken. They were delicious meals but I am now eating less fat and choosing healthier ways to prepare foods. The dish I am sharing for Bless This Table is one of my favorites. It is chicken with onions, potatoes and sauerkraut. It is a Black and Native American recipe from Oklahoma that became popular because it is a one-pot dish. I have included a vegetable salad with a vinaigrette which goes beautifully with this dish. I hope this meal will become one of your favorites, too.

CHICKEN, ONIONS, POTATOES AND SAUERKRAUT

INGREDIENTS

Chicken (6 to 8 Pieces)

1 onion, sliced

Spike™ seasoning salt

Fresh ground black pepper

6 potatoes (peeled & quartered)

2 cloves garlic (minced or pressed)

1 (32-ounce) jar of sauerkraut, drained

1 cup of water or chicken stock

DIRECTIONS

You will need a large size heavy cast iron pot with a lid.

Season each individual piece of chicken with Spike™ seasoning salt.

Arrange the chicken on the bottom of the pot.

Season the potatoes with Spike™ and add to pot with onion and fresh crushed garlic.

Drain the sauerkraut and add lots of fresh ground pepper. Put sauerkraut in the pot.

On top of all the ingredients, pour in water or chicken stock.

Boil for 15 minutes, then cover pot. Simmer for 45 minutes.

Top with lots of extra fresh ground black pepper to taste.

GARDEN VEGETABLE SALAD WITH VINAIGRETTE

INGREDIENTS

1 bag salad greens of choice

1 cucumber, peeled and sliced

1 red pepper, cut into 1-inch pieces

1 avocado, sliced

Small container of cherry tomatoes

VINAIGRETTE INGREDIENTS

3 tablespoons Dijon mustard

6 tablespoons white wine vinegar

1 cup olive oil

1 teaspoon sugar (optional)

Salt and pepper, to taste

DIRECTIONS FOR SALAD

Combine all ingredients in a large bowl.

Add vinaigrette dressing to coat leaves lightly.

Toss and serve.

DIRECTIONS FOR VINAIGRETTE

Whisk together the Dijon mustard and white wine vinegar. Slowly add the olive oil. Add sugar, salt and pepper. Blend well.

Reba

Reba is one of the most successful Country recording artists of all time, celebrating an amazing thirty-five #1 hit singles. She is an accomplished actress in film, stage and television. Her hit TV series, *Reba*, garnered her a Golden Globe nomination and People's Choice Award. She also has her own clothing line, home collection, footwear and luggage.

⌒ FAMILY MEAL ⌒

BAKED VEGETABLES

OR

CHICKEN WITH BAKED VEGETABLES

Family time is so important. No matter where you are, gathering around the table with family and friends is a rich experience to cherish. For Bless This Table, I am sharing a fabulous chicken and vegetables recipe. The good news about this dish is that it not only tastes incredible but it is a healthy guilt free dish. I hope you will enjoy this meal with your family that I share with you with love.

BAKED VEGETABLES OR CHICKEN WITH BAKED VEGETABLES

INGREDIENTS

Wash and prepare:

4 new potatoes (cut in half long ways)

1 yellow onion (cut in chunks)

1 purple onion (cut in chunks)

1 white or Vidalia onion (cut in chunks)

1 sweet potato (cut in chunks)

1 yellow pepper
(cut in long slices and then in half)

1 red pepper
(cut in long slices and then in half)

1 green pepper
(cut in long slices and then in half)

Fresh green beans
(take off ends and snap in half)

Garlic (as many cloves as you want.
I like a lot!)

Baby carrots (as many as you like)

1/3 cup olive oil

Broccoli

1 stick butter

Cauliflower

½ cup Chardonnay wine

Salt and pepper, to taste

4 chicken breasts – skin on, (optional)

You can substitute or delete any of these vegetables. Just make sure you have colorful vegetables. It looks better!

DIRECTIONS

In a roasting pan, pour the olive oil in the bottom, an "S" will be fine.

As you are cutting the vegetables, go ahead and place them in the roasting pan. Mix them so the color will look good.

Take a stick of butter, cut chunks off and place it here and there over and in the vegetables.

Pour Chardonnay wine over the vegetables.

Salt and pepper to taste, not too much.

Do not cover.

Cook for one hour at 400 degrees.

If you want to add chicken and make it a one pan meal:

Take 4 chicken breasts with the skin and rinse them off.

Place them in the vegetables and cook for one hour at 400 degrees.

You can remove the skin before you serve. The skin just keeps the chicken more moist.

Reba's Blessing

Thank you so much for this time

with family and friends.

Bless this food we are about to eat

with nourishment and light,

and may this meal together

bring us all closer to each other in love.

Thank you for our good health and

all the countless fortunes in our lives.

Amen.

Richard Marx

Singer Richard Marx's debut album sold 3 million copies – he has since gone on to sell over 30 million albums and has received numerous awards along the way. As a producer/songwriter he has co-written songs with top recording artists from Luther Vandross, 'N Sync, Keith Urban to Barbra Streisand to name a few. Through these collaborations and his own hit singles as an artist, he has amazingly penned fourteen #1 songs.

From very early in Richard's career he has participated in many charities supporting children through the Children of the Night Foundation, Toys For Tots, Ronald McDonald House, Best Buddies, The Special Olympics and Make A Wish Foundation. Additionally, he organizes and performs at an annual benefit concert for Cystic Fibrosis.

 FAMILY MEAL

RUTH'S STUFFED PEPPERS

CYNTHIA'S KITCHEN SINK SALAD

CYNTHIA'S HOMEMADE OATMEAL CHOCOLATE CHIP COOKIES

Although I was an only child, family dinner was very important to the three members of the Marx family in Highland Park, Illinois. My dad ran his own jingle company in downtown Chicago and my mother sang on many of the jingles he composed and produced, as did I. As busy as they were, my parents were home for dinner nearly every night. We rarely ate out at restaurants, and my mom seemed to use cooking as a decompression from her day in the studio. We would sit at the kitchen table, eat dinner, and talk about everything under the sun. The close and loving bond I had with my folks was fueled by those talks over dinner.

I was a very finicky eater until I was around eighteen, but I had one dish my mother cooked once or twice a year that I called my favorite. Stuffed peppers. In reality, it was only the stuffing I ate when I was a kid. I avoided the peppers like they were rat droppings. But as an adult, it's the combination of flavors that still make it one of my favorite meals, and I devour every sliver of those peppers. The best part is that my mom, healthy and active at 75, still makes them for me.

My family and I also made dinner a ritual since our three sons were born. Only our youngest, seventeen year old Jesse, is still living at home, but we still make a point to have dinner together as much as we can. My wife, Cynthia, is the first to admit she's no Julia Child, but she tries. We both try to eat clean, and lean. Part of the reason for that is so we can occasionally indulge in our mutual love of dark chocolate. And nothing beats Cynthia's homemade oatmeal chocolate chip cookies.

Richard Marx

RUTH'S STUFFED PEPPERS

INGREDIENTS

6 large green peppers

2 cups brown rice

2 pounds ground turkey

1 bottle of smoked bbq sauce

INGREDIENTS FOR SAUCE

2 (14-ounce) cans tomato sauce

½ (6-ounce) can tomato paste

1 heaping tablespoon sugar

¼ cup red wine

1 (8-ounce) can of petite diced tomatoes, plain

2 cloves garlic, minced

DIRECTIONS

Preheat oven to 375 degrees.

Take 6 large green peppers.

Clean and cut tops off and remove seeds.

Put in boiling water and blanch 5 minutes.

Place in pre-sprayed casserole dish with tops off.

Cook 2 cups brown rice according to package directions-do not overcook.

Set aside.

In a large skillet, cook ground turkey until brown.

Add cooked rice to meat.

Add ½ to ¾ bottle of smoked bbq sauce.

Stir well.

Drop meat mixture into peppers, packed loosely, do not press down-leave ½ inch above top.

Drop extra meat stuffing to surround peppers.

Pour sauce over peppers and cover with foil and bake for 45 minutes.

Test with fork-if pepper is easily penetrated, it's ready.

CYNTHIA'S KITCHEN SINK SALAD

INGREDIENTS

1 bag of baby spinach or mixed lettuce

1 bag of mixed fresh veggies (carrots, broccoli, cauliflower)

1 red apple, cored

1 (7-ounce) bag of glazed walnuts or pecans

1 container of blue cheese or goat cheese with herbs

¼ cup raisins

¼ cup of dried cranberries

Favorite dressing: Low Fat Raspberry Balsamic vinaigrette

DIRECTIONS

Chop first 4 ingredients with hand chopper (you can add whatever additional veggies you like).

Once chopped, mix in last three ingredients.

Add favorite dressing and serve.

CYNTHIA'S HOMEMADE OATMEAL CHOCOLATE CHIP COOKIES

INGREDIENTS

1 ¼ cups flour

½ cup white sugar

¾ cup brown sugar

1 teaspoon baking soda

1 teaspoon cinnamon

1 teaspoon salt

½ teaspoon nutmeg

2 ½ sticks salted butter, melted

1 teaspoon vanilla

1 egg

1 and ½ cups old fashioned oats

1 bag semi sweet chocolate chips

DIRECTIONS

Preheat oven to 375 degrees.

In a large bowl, stir dry ingredients.

In an additional large bowl, mix wet ingredients.

Add wet mixture to dry mixture and stir well.

Add oats and chips and stir thoroughly.

Spoon out cookie dough on ungreased cookie sheet in 3 inch rounds.

Bake for 10 minutes and watch to see when cookies are golden brown at edges. May need to cook up to an additional 3 minutes depending on oven.

Remove from oven and allow to cool 2 minutes on cookie sheet before transferring to a wire rack.

Rita Wilson

Rita Wilson is an accomplished motion picture, television and stage actress (*It's Complicated, Sleepless In Seattle, The Good Wife, Chicago*), film producer (she discovered the Oscar nominated *My Big Fat Greek Wedding* and *Mamma Mia!*), and has most recently added "recording artist" to her list of accomplishments, with the release of her debut album *AM/FM* on Decca Records. She also devotes considerable energy and support to many worthy charities, with particular focus on medical research and children's causes.

 FAMILY MEAL

RITA'S BURRITOS

LEMON BREAD

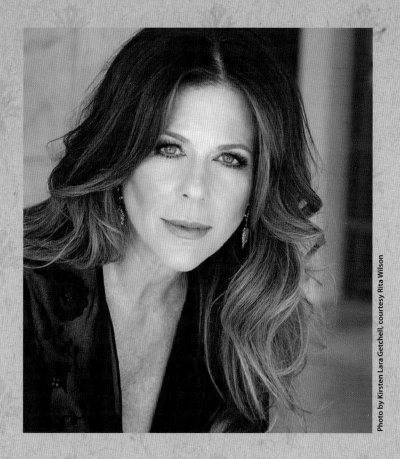

We believe in family dinner. It's the time that we all get to catch up on the day. We play "High Point / Low Point" to see what went well that day, or what could have gone better. It's a great way to let the kids know that even adults have things each day that could have gone better. Family dinner has been one of the best things for us. There's nothing like it. —Rita

RITA'S BURRITOS

INGREDIENTS

1 pound ground beef

1 small can diced green chilis

1 (16-ounce) can refried beans

4 to 5 flour tortillas, burrito size

Cheddar cheese, shredded

Butter

DIRECTIONS

Brown the ground beef in a skillet.

Drain the fat.

Add chilis and beans and mix together.

Fill a tortilla with mixture and add cheese.

Brush the tortilla with butter inside and out.

Fold over the edges.

Bake in 400 degree oven for 20 minutes or until crisp.

LEMON BREAD

INGREDIENTS

⅓ cup butter, melted

1 cup sugar

3 tablespoons lemon extract

2 eggs

1 ½ cups sifted flour

1 teaspoon baking powder

1 teaspoon salt

½ cup milk

2 tablespoons grated lemon rind

ICING:

¼ cup lemon juice

½ cup sugar

DIRECTIONS

Preheat oven to 350 degrees. Grease and flour a 9" loaf pan.

In a large bowl, mix the butter, 1 cup of sugar and the lemon extract. Beat the eggs into the butter mixture.

In a separate bowl, sift together the flour, baking powder and salt. Add the flour to the butter mixture alternately with the milk, beating just enough to blend. Fold in the lemon rind. Pour batter into loaf pan.

Bake for 1 hour or until toothpick comes out clean. Cool 10 minutes and remove from the pan.

Mix the lemon juice and sugar together.

While the bread is still hot, pour the lemon mixture over the top and into any cracks formed while baking.

When cool, wrap tightly in foil and store for 24 hours before slicing.

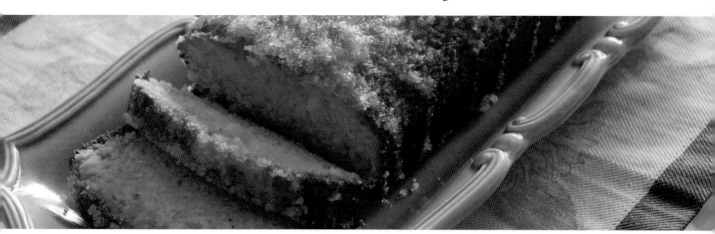

The Cox Family

The Cox Family are celebrated recording artists that have uniquely combined the sound of Bluegrass, Country and Gospel in their music. They have won numerous awards including 5 Grammys. The family also appeared in the movie, *Oh Brother Where Art Thou?*

～ FAMILY MEAL ～

CHICKEN AND DRESSING

SWEET POTATOES
WITH MARSHMALLOW TOPPING

BROCCOLI, CHEESE AND RICE CASSEROLE

POTATO SALAD

SWEET POTATO PIE

Photo by Karen Miller, courtesy The Cox Family

Louisiana cooking is legendary for it's eclectic spices and savory courses. Our native cuisine, tends to capture it's fame from the flame some might say. However growing up in north Louisiana, modesty still is the gustation for most. Although my mother's ancestry is of French decent, not every meal she prepared was intrinsic with respect to the use of hot peppers. In fact, creole was second, as an all time family favorite to her chicken and dressing. For this annual Thanksgiving, Christmas, or Easter entrée, she would solicit the help of my father, as I recall, in the rendering and final seasoning. And, for as many years as they shared in the making of this traditional recipe, they also reflected on the times past when my grandma Cox had been the keeper of such a fine family secret. That was of course until June 1958, the year Mama and Daddy were married.

MARIE COX'S CHICKEN AND DRESSING

INGREDIENTS

2 9-inch skillets of cornbread

4 homemade biscuits

4 slices of white bread

3 eggs

2 sticks of butter

1 4½ pound hen boiled (save the broth)

1 tablespoon of sage seasoning

1 tablespoon of poultry seasoning

Salt and pepper, to taste

3 stalks of celery, finely chopped

1 large white onion, minced

DIRECTIONS

Put hen in large pot and cover with water. Season with salt and pepper.

When water comes to a gentle boil, continue cooking for 45 minutes to an hour.

De-bone and cut up into pieces and save the broth.

Mix breads together and add 6 to 7 cups of broth (make sure the broth is warm so the butter will melt).

Add onions and celery.

Add both sticks of butter.

Add sage and poultry seasoning.

Add eggs.

Mix together well.

Pour into 1 large roasting pan, similar to what you would roast a turkey.

Place pieces of chicken into the dressing.

Bake at 350 degrees for 45 minutes or until brown.

Will feed 10 people with leftovers.

SWEET POTATOES
(WITH MARSHMALLOW TOPPING)

INGREDIENTS

6 cups of peeled sweet potatoes, quartered

2 cups of sugar

1 teaspoon salt

4 eggs

1 stick of butter

1 cup of evaporated milk

1½ teaspoon of vanilla

1 bag miniature marshmallows

DIRECTIONS

Boil potatoes until tender when pierced with a fork.

Add potatoes to large bowl and blend with a mixer.

Add all other ingredients, except marshmallows and blend until smooth.

Pour in 9"x13" inch pan.

Bake at 350 degrees for 55 minutes.

Insert knife or toothpick in middle to check when done. Take out and increase oven temperature to 450 degrees.

Pour miniature marshmallows on top. Put back into oven. Bake until brown.

BROCCOLI, CHEESE AND RICE CASSEROLE

INGREDIENTS

½ cup onion, chopped

½ cup celery, chopped

1 (10-ounce) package frozen chopped broccoli, thawed

1 tablespoon butter

1 (8-ounce) jar cheese spread

1 (10.75-ounce) can condensed cream of mushroom soup

1 (5-ounce) can evaporated milk

3 cups cooked rice

DIRECTIONS

In a large skillet over medium heat, sauté onion, celery and broccoli in butter for 3 to 5 minutes.

Stir in cheese, soup, and milk until smooth.

Place rice in greased 8-inch square baking dish.

Pour cheese mixture over rice, do not stir.

Bake uncovered at 325 degrees for 25 to 30 minutes or until hot and bubbly.

If everyone was going to be there, we doubled the recipe!

POTATO SALAD

INGREDIENTS

10 peeled potatoes, cut into chunks

5 hard boiled eggs, roughly chopped

½ cup dill pickle relish or chopped dill pickles

¾ cup mayonnaise

1 tablespoon mustard, or to taste

Salt and black pepper, to taste

½ cup purple onion, finely chopped, optional*

DIRECTIONS

Place the potatoes in a large pot. Cover them with water and bring to a boil over high heat.

Reduce the heat to medium-low, and simmer until the potatoes are cooked through but still firm, about 20 minutes.

Remove from the water. Set the potatoes aside.

In a bowl, stir together the mayonnaise, mustard, pickles, salt and pepper until well mixed.

Place the potatoes and eggs in a large salad bowl.

Pour the mixture over the potatoes and eggs and mix lightly. Cover and refrigerate the salad.

*Two bowls of potato salad were traditionally made, one for those that liked onions and one for those who didn't. If you like it with onions – add finely chopped purple onion.

SWEET POTATO PIE

INGREDIENTS

2 cups cooked, mashed sweet potatoes

1 stick butter, softened

2 eggs

1 ¼ cups sugar

1 teaspoon vanilla

½ teaspoon cinnamon

½ teaspoon nutmeg

1 large can evaporated milk

2 unbaked pie shells

DIRECTIONS

Beat cooked sweet potatoes with electric mixer.

Add softened butter, eggs, and sugar to hot potatoes.

Beat well; discard all potato mixture left on beaters.

Beat 2 more times and discard all left on beaters (this takes out all strings).

Add spices and vanilla; beat well.

Add evaporated milk; beat well.

Pour into unbaked pie shells.

Bake in a preheated 350 degree oven for 45 to 50 minutes or until a knife inserted into center comes out clean.

This mixture is very thin but it will make a delicious, creamy pie and will stay moist.

Willard Cox's Blessing

Our Father we come before you today

with humble hearts.

Thanking you for the blessings you've given us.

We ask that you will continue to bless this family

and the families across this land.

Lets us not forget the sacrifice that the boys

made to keep this land free

for us to partake in this special dinner.

Continue to bless us in your most holy name, Amen!

The Pointer Sisters

The Pointer Sisters are internationally known recording artists and theatrical performers. Their multi-platinum albums were recorded over the span of three decades and have earned them 3 Grammy Awards. They are one of the rare acts who have achieved having top hits on the Pop, R&B and Country charts simultaneously.

 FAMILY MEAL

CHICKEN AND DUMPLIN'S

TAMALE PIE

1234 CAKE

Photo by Norman Seeff, courtesy The Pointer Sisters

Elton and Sarah Pointer had six children, Aaron, Fritz, Ruth, Anita, Patricia and June, so there was a lot of cookin' goin' on every day by Mom at our house. On special occasions whether it was Mothers Day, Fathers Day, Easter or Christmas we all had a speech to give at church and we would be rewarded with a great meal at home.

I have so many great memories of Mother, Sister Lee and Aunt Clara Mae in the kitchen preparing holiday dinners. They sure were great cooks! I can remember thinking even then as a young woman, who will carry this on when Mom is gone. Holiday dinners will never be the same. I really miss those wonderful times.

Anita Pointer

CHICKEN AND DUMPLIN'S

INGREDIENTS

1 whole chicken

1 large onion, chopped

Salt and pepper

3 cups flour

Pinch of salt (for dumplin's)

2 eggs

½ cup cold water (can add more if needed to stiffen the flour)

Clove garlic, minced (optional)*

DIRECTIONS

Put chicken in large pot. Add water to pot, enough to cover chicken. Cook on high heat. Add onion, salt and pepper to the chicken.

When water begins to boil, lower temperature and continue to cook until chicken is tender. This usually takes about 40 to 45 minutes.

In large bowl, add flour and salt. With a fork, beat eggs in small bowl and add to flour with the cold water. Spoon onto floured board and roll smooth. Cut into 2 inch squares.

You can leave the chicken in the pot or remove it when you add the dumplin's. Make sure the broth is boiling when you add the dumplin's. Once they are fully cooked, you can add the chicken back to the pot.

*I add a clove of minced garlic to the chicken but the original recipe from my mother only used onions.

Recipe from Mother, Sarah Pointer

TAMALE PIE

INGREDIENTS

1 ½ cups corn meal

Cold water for paste

1 or 2 lbs of ground turkey or ground beef

1 tablespoon chili powder

¼ - ½ cup tomato sauce

Pinch of salt

DIRECTIONS

Mix corn meal into cold water to form paste.

Spoon into 2 cups boiling water and add a pinch of salt.

Sauté ground turkey or ground beef in skillet until brown.

Add chili powder.

Add small amount of tomato sauce, ¼ cup to ½ cup to meat depending on amount of meat that you use.

Cook until done.

Mix small amount of meat to corn meal paste (should be thick -not stiff).

Oil casserole dish.

Add layer of corn meal.

Then add layer of meat, layer of corn meal.

Layer of meat.

Bake at 350 degrees for ½ hour to 45 minutes until crust is firm.

Recipe from Mother, Sarah Pointer

1234 CAKE

INGREDIENTS	DIRECTIONS
1 cup of shortening or butter	Cream sugar and shortening or butter.
2 cups of sugar	Add eggs.
3 cups of flour	Add milk.
4 eggs	Sift flour with baking powder and a pinch of salt.
2 teaspoons baking powder	Add a little at a time to butter sugar mixture.
2 teaspoons vanilla	Add vanilla.
1 cup milk	Grease and flour bundt pan.
Pinch of salt	Bake at 350 degrees for 1 hour and 15 minutes until top is lightly brown and firm to touch.

If preparing for a layer cake, grease and flour two 9 inch round pans. Bake for 30 minutes.

This was the first cake I learned how to bake. GrandMa Roxie taught me this recipe when I was in the fifth grade, living with her in Arkansas. – A.P.

Mother and Anita's Blessing

Our loving Father,

We want to thank you for today.

Thank you for your love, kindness and tender mercy.

Thank you for those praying for us.

Thank you for those we're praying for.

God bless this food.

May it nourish our bodies.

In the name of God we pray, Amen.

Vince Gill & Amy Grant

Vince Gill is a Country singer, songwriter and musician who has sold more than 26 million records. He has won 18 CMA Awards, 20 Grammy Awards and has been inducted into the Country Music Hall Of Fame. Vince is regarded as one of Country Music's truest humanitarians, having participated in hundreds of charitable events throughout his career.

Amy Grant is best known for her Gospel and Contemporary Christian music, having sold over 30 million records worldwide and having received 6 Grammys and numerous Dove Awards. She has also succeeded in the pop market where she had a #1 single, "Baby Baby" and is an accomplished author.

～ FAMILY MEAL ～

CHICKEN SALAD

CAJUN GREENS

CORN SOUFFLE

BLACK EYED PEAS

GRANT'S PECAN HALVES

Photo by Kristin Barlowe, courtesy Vince Gill and Amy Grant

One of the most memorable experiences of holiday gatherings for our family is traditional food that is prepared for each celebration. Amy is sharing her corn souffle with Bless This Table that is one of our favorite dishes prepared for our Thanksgiving table every year. Amy's parents, Burton and Gloria, traditionally made the pecan halves for Christmas gifts for their friends and of course, we could hardly wait to get our batch! The Cajun Greens and Black Eyed Peas are made every New Year's Day. I don't think you could find a tastier version than the recipes we are sharing with you. Lastly, we are including Gloria's treasured secret recipe for chicken salad. We hope that when you prepare these dishes you will feel the comfort in this food that we have been blessed to experience.

Vince

CHICKEN SALAD

INGREDIENTS

1 whole chicken

1 large can chicken broth

1 bunch of celery

3 cans of crushed pineapple
(No. 2 can size)

1 jar mayonnaise

DIRECTIONS

Boil chicken in chicken broth for extra flavor.

Debone chicken and cut up with scissors into bite size pieces in a large bowl.

Dice celery.

Add pineapple that has been drained thoroughly.

Mix your ingredients together.

Now add 1 cup of mayo at a time. Taste as you go along. You can add mayo until you get the right texture/taste for you.

This is a famous recipe of Gloria Grant, Amy's mother.

CAJUN GREENS

INGREDIENTS

2 bundles of greens (1 of kale and 1 of mustard or collard)

1 (14.5-ounce) can stewed tomatoes (juice and all)

1 jalapeno (drop in whole with small slice down the middle)

Bacon ends, ½ the package cut up in small pieces

1 large onion

1 garlic clove

2 teaspoons ham base

1 teaspoon Cajun seasoning

2 cups water

Black pepper, to taste

1 bay leaf and remove before serving

DIRECTIONS

Sauté bacon and onion together until lightly browned.

Add jalapeno, garlic and tomatoes.

Sauté 5 minutes more.

Add all the other ingredients and stir well.

Bring to a boil, then cover and reduce to simmer for 3 hours with lid askew.

CORN SOUFFLE

INGREDIENTS

1 (8-ounce) can regular corn (drained)

1 (8-ounce) can creamed corn

1 cup sour cream

2 eggs

1 box (8-ounce) corn muffin mix

1 stick butter

DIRECTIONS

Melt butter and mix with corn muffin mix.

Stir in both corns and sour cream.

Beat eggs slightly. Mix together with other ingredients using a wire whisk.

Pour into 1½ quart casserole.

Bake at 350 degrees for 1 hour or until center is set.

BLACK EYED PEAS

INGREDIENTS

4 cans of black eyed peas

3 stalks of celery

1 garlic clove

1 large onion

Bacon ends, ½ of the package cut in small pieces

Salt and pepper, to taste

1 dried red pepper, broken up

¼ teaspoon cayenne

Enough water to just cover the peas

DIRECTIONS

Sauté onion and bacon until lightly browned.

Add garlic and celery and dried red pepper. Sauté 5 more minutes.

Add everything else and bring to a boil, then reduce to a simmer. Continue cooking uncovered for 2 hours.

GRANT'S PECAN HALVES

INGREDIENTS

1 cup of pecans

½ cup of sugar

2 tablespoons butter

½ teaspoon vanilla

Salt to taste

DIRECTIONS

In an iron skillet, melt butter, add sugar and vanilla. Let the sugar brown and quickly add the pecans.

Stir and remove from the heat.

After mixing really well, spread the mixture on a sheet of foil. Salt to taste.

Let cool and then break up and place in a bowl for serving.

Wolfgang Puck

The name Wolfgang Puck is synonymous with the best of restaurant hospitality and the ultimate in all aspects of the culinary arts. He is an award-winning chef, celebrated restaurateur, philanthropist, author and Emmy winner. He has gone from his homeland, Austria, to the culinary world-wide stage. Wolfgang's vast consumer products include his all natural signature hand-crafted pizzas and branded housewares.

 FAMILY MEAL

WIENER BACKHENDL (FRIED CHICKEN)

MY GRANDMA'S RAVIOLI

MY MOTHER'S GARDEN VEGETABLE SOUP

APRICOT PALATSCHINKEN

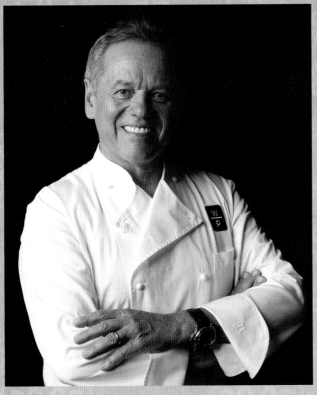

Photo by Amanda Marsalis, courtesy Wolfgang Puck

Growing up in a place where there was no fast food whatsoever, my mother's cooking was certainly the greatest food for all. Every meal – breakfast, lunch and dinner – was eaten at home. Thank God my mom was a fabulous cook. She was a professional cook during the summertime and the rest of the year, she spent cooking every meal for us. I remember us kids fighting for her wonderful cheese raviolis and especially her great desserts. We had competitions to see who could eat more palatschinken – but my father always won because he ate faster than the rest of us. The Viennese-style fried chicken, or backhendl as we call it, was always a great treat for special occasions.

WIENER BACKHENDL
(FRIED CHICKEN)

INGREDIENTS

1 2½ pound chicken

2 cups flour

3 eggs

4 cups of panko or bread crumbs

Vegetable oil for frying

Salt and pepper

2 lemons

1 cup of parsley leaves

DIRECTIONS

Cut chicken into 8 pieces. Remove skin but not the bones. Season generously with salt and pepper.

Heat vegetable oil to 300 degrees.

On 3 separate soup plates, put the flour, eggs and bread crumbs, and dip all chicken pieces first in flour, then eggs, and finally bread crumbs. Shake off excess crumbs.

Fry chicken pieces for about 12 to 14 minutes until nice and brown. Drain on paper towels.

Fry the parsley for about 30 seconds. Remove, drain on paper towels and sprinkle over chicken.

Divide onto 4 plates. Sprinkle with parsley and serve with half a lemon.

In Vienna, fried chicken is always served with a salad of mixed greens, cucumbers, tomatoes, potatoes, etc. I must say, as a kid, I preferred mashed potatoes.

Yield: Serves 4

MY GRANDMA'S RAVIOLI

INGREDIENTS

1 pound baking potatoes (about 2 large), scrubbed thoroughly

2 tablespoons (¼ stick) unsalted butter

2 tablespoons minced shallots

1 teaspoon minced garlic

8 ounces farmer cheese

5 ounces goat cheese

2 ounces mascarpone cheese

3 tablespoons freshly grated Parmesan cheese

2 tablespoons minced fresh mint leaves

2 tablespoons minced fresh chervil leaves

1 egg, slightly beaten

Kosher salt and freshly ground white pepper

BASIC PASTA DOUGH INGREDIENTS

Semolina or all-purpose flour, for dusting

1 egg lightly beaten with 1 teaspoon water, for egg wash

8 tablespoons (1 stick) unsalted butter

¼ cup freshly grated Parmesan cheese

Kosher salt and freshly ground white pepper

Minced fresh flat-leaf parsley leaves

DIRECTIONS

Make the filling: Bake the potatoes in a preheated 350 degree oven until fork tender, about 30 to 40 minutes. Peel, and while still warm, pass through a food mill. In a small sauté pan, heat the butter over medium heat. Add the shallots and garlic and cook until soft. In a medium bowl, combine all the cheeses, the herbs and the beaten egg.

Add the cooked shallots and garlic and the warm potato. Stir until blended (being careful not to overmix, or the mixture will get pasty). Season with salt and pepper. Cover and refrigerate until needed. Then, with lightly moistened hands, roll into ½-ounce balls, about the size of golf balls.

Cut the pasta dough into 4 portions and work with 1 portion at a time, keeping the remaining dough covered with plastic wrap. Lightly dust the work surface with flour. With a pasta machine or a rolling pin, roll out the dough about 20 inches long and 4 inches wide. Brush the dough with egg wash and arrange 9 to 10 balls of filling on the lower third of the length of the dough, about 1 to 1-½ inches apart.

Fold the top half over to cover the balls. Press the dough around each ball to seal, making sure that you do not have any air pockets. With a 2-inch round cookie cutter, cut the ravioli. Dust a tray with flour and arrange the ravioli on the tray, dusting with more flour. Repeat with the remaining dough, egg wash, and filling. Refrigerate, covered, until needed.

Bring a large pot of salted water to a boil.

Cook the ravioli until al dente, about 3 to 4 minutes.

Meanwhile, in a large sauté pan, over high heat, cook the butter until it begins to brown.

Drain the ravioli and toss into the browned butter, turning to coat both sides. Add the cheese and season with salt and pepper.

Garnish with parsley and serve immediately.

Makes 36 to 40 ravioli.

MY MOTHER'S GARDEN VEGETABLE SOUP

INGREDIENTS

2 small leeks (*white parts only, split lengthwise, thoroughly washed with cold running water, patted dry, and diced*)

1 small onion, peeled and diced

2 stalks celery, diced

2 medium carrots, peeled

1 large potato, peeled and diced

1 medium zucchini, trimmed and diced

12 green beans, trimmed and diced

6 tablespoons olive oil

3 tablespoons water

2 quarts good-quality canned or home made chicken broth, beef broth, or vegetable broth

Salt

6 ripe tomatoes, peeled and seeded

30 fresh basil leaves, washed and dried

4 medium garlic cloves, peeled

Freshly ground black pepper

DIRECTIONS

Cut the leeks, onion, celery, carrots, potato, zucchini and green beans into ¼-inch dice.

In a 6-quart (6-1) stockpot, combine 3 tablespoons of the olive oil with the 3 tablespoons of water. Add the diced leeks and onion and sauté over medium-low heat until all the water evaporates and the vegetables are tender but not yet beginning to brown, about 5 minutes.

Add the celery, potato, carrots, zucchini, and broth, and season to taste with salt. Raise the heat to high and bring the broth to a boil. Reduce the heat to maintain a gentle boil and cook, uncovered, for 30 minutes.

Meanwhile, bring a medium saucepan of water to a boil and fill a bowl nearby with ice cubes and water. With a small, sharp knife, cut out the cores of the tomatoes and score a shallow X in the skin on the opposite side. With a slotted spoon, lower the tomatoes into the boiling water and boil until the skin begins to wrinkle, 20 to 30 seconds. Remove the tomatoes with the slotted spoon to the ice water. When the tomatoes are cool enough to handle, peel off their skins, using the knife to help if necessary. Halve the tomatoes and squeeze out their seeds. Coarsely chop the tomatoes.

In a food processor fitted with the metal blade, put the tomatoes, basil, garlic, and remaining 3 tablespoons olive oil. Pulse the machine until the vegetables are pureed to make a pistou. Transfer to a sauceboat or bowl and set aside.

About 5 minutes before the soup is done, stir the diced green beans into the pot and continue cooking until all the vegetables are tender.

Season the cooked soup to taste with more salt and black pepper to taste. Stir the pistou into the cooked soup or pass the pistou separately for each person to add to taste. Ladle the soup into a tureen or individual bowls and serve.

APRICOT PALATSCHINKEN

INGREDIENTS

1 cage-free egg

2/3 cup milk

1 teaspoon sugar

Pinch of salt

½ cup plus 2 tablespoons all-purpose flour

3 tablespoons heavy cream

1 tablespoon butter (for pan)

APRICOT COMPOTE:

1 pound of organic apricots, locally grown, (about 6 medium), sliced in eighths

½ cup sugar

½ vanilla bean, scraped, or 2 teaspoons vanilla extract

4 tablespoons orange juice

1 tablespoon lemon juice

Powdered sugar for dusting

DIRECTIONS

In a small stainless steel mixing bowl, whisk together the egg, milk, sugar, salt, flour and cream creating a smooth batter. Strain. Let rest in the refrigerator, covered with plastic, for one hour. (Or, can be made the day before).

Remove from refrigerator. Stir the batter and add any flavoring.

Brush a 12 inch Teflon frying pan with butter and heat. Ladle approximately 1 ounce of batter into pan, twirling by hand in a circular motion to create a very thin crepe. Cook crepe until golden, approximately 1 minute on each side.

In a medium saucepan, combine the sugar, scraped vanilla bean, orange juice and lemon juice. Bring to a boil. Add the 6 sliced apricots and cook for 2 to 3 minutes.

Presentation: Put 2 tablespoons of the apricot preserves into a crepe. Roll the crepe or fold it in half twice to make a quarter. Dust with powdered sugar.

Makes 24, for 8 to 12 people.

Wynonna

Five-time Grammy Award winning artist, Wynonna Judd, first gained fame as part of one of the most successful musical duos of all time, The Judds. On top of that accomplishment, she also holds multiple gold, platinum and multi-platinum certifications from the RIAA in excess of 30 million albums sold worldwide throughout her illustrious 30-year career. In addition to her countless musical achievements, Wynonna is also a New York Times best-selling author, accomplished actress and tireless humanitarian.

FAMILY MEAL

CHICKEN POT PIE

Photo by Kristin Barlowe, courtesy Wynonna

Ashley and I grew up in Kentucky on a mountaintop. We spent years on welfare and our single working mother, Naomi, was often gone working 2-3 jobs to make ends meet. This kind of comfort food is my favorite because it was made with love from scratch. It brings back memories of us all sitting around the supper table together. Though we had very little, materialistically, I feel we had everything because we had each other. Family is everything. Homemade food is the bonus!

Love
Wynonna

CHICKEN POT PIE

PIE CRUST INGREDIENTS

3 cups all-purpose flour

1 teaspoon salt

1 cup solid vegetable shortening

1 large egg

1 tablespoon distilled white vinegar

4 to 5 tablespoons ice water

CHICKEN FILLING INGREDIENTS

1 whole chicken (about 3 ½ pounds), giblets and liver removed for other uses

2 medium all-purpose potatoes, peeled and cut into ¾-inch chunks

3 medium carrots, trimmed and sliced ¼ inch thick

2 stalks celery, trimmed and sliced ¼ inch thick

1 medium onion, diced

1 can (10.75-ounce) condensed cream of chicken soup, undiluted

1 container (16-ounce) sour cream

1 can (8 ½-ounce) tiny green peas, drained

½ teaspoon salt

½ teaspoon black pepper

DIRECTIONS FOR PIE CRUST

In a large bowl, stir together the flour and salt.

Using a pastry blender or 2 knives used like scissors, cut in the shortening until the mixture resembles coarse crumbs.

In a small bowl, mix together the egg, vinegar, and 4 tablespoons of the ice water.

Drizzle over the flour mixture, tossing with a fork, until the dough comes together (if the dough seems a little dry, add the remaining tablespoon of water).

With your hands, press the dough into a ball. Divide into 2 pieces, one slightly larger than the other.

Flatten into 2 disks, 1 inch thick. Wrap each in plastic wrap and refrigerate for at least 30 minutes.

MEANWHILE, MAKE THE CHICKEN FILLING

Place the chicken in a 6-quart pot. Cover with cold water and bring to a boil.

Lower the heat and simmer until the thigh meat of the chicken is no longer pink near the bone, about 45 minutes.

Remove the chicken from the pot. Reserve the cooking liquid.

Bring the cooking liquid to a boil over medium-high heat.

Add the potato, carrot, celery, and onion. Return to the boil and cook until the potato chunks are just tender and still hold their shape, about 10 minutes.

Drain, reserving the cooking liquid for soup making or for other uses.

When the chicken is cool enough to handle, remove the skin and bones and discard. Cut the chicken meat into bite-size pieces.

In a large bowl, stir together the soup and sour cream.

Fold in the chicken and the vegetables, including the peas. Stir in the salt and pepper.

Preheat the oven to 350°.

ROLL OUT THE DOUGH:
On a lightly floured surface, with a lightly floured rolling pin, roll out the larger disk of dough into a 13-inch circle.

Ease the circle into a 9-inch deep-dish pie plate. Gently press the dough against the sides and bottom of the plate.

Trim the edges to a ¾-inch overhang.

Roll out the remaining dough into a 12-inch circle and drape it over the rolling pin.

TO ASSEMBLE THE PIE:
Spoon the chicken filling into the crust-lined pie plate, mounding it in the center.

Unroll the dough from the rolling pin over the filling.

Seal the edges together and flute. Cut several steam vents in the top of the pie.

Place a sheet of aluminum foil on the bottom rack in the oven to catch any drips.

Bake the pie in the 350 degree oven until the crust is lightly golden and the filling is bubbly, about 1 hour and 45 minutes.

Transfer the pie to a wire rack and let stand for 20 minutes before serving.

TIP: You can cut out little chickens, stars, or other shapes from the dough with cookie cutters and place them on top of the crust.

Wynonna's Blessing

Father,

Bless this food to the nourishment of our bodies.

Thank you for our family and friends.

Please keep us mindful of those in need.

In Jesus' name we pray, Amen.

Your Family's Story

Your Family's Recipes

Your Family's Recipes

Your Family's Recipes

Your Family's Blessing

Notes

Index

A

Alma's Italian Cream Cake 32

Almonds; 65, 86

Antipasto 78

APPETIZERS:
  Stuffed Vine Leaves 36
  Antipasto 78
  Knishes, Audrey's Famous Cheese 52

Apricot Palatschinken 143

Apricots; 143

Artichokes; 78

Asparagus; 80

Avocados; 99

B

Baby Lima Beans 44

Bacon; 16, 89, 131, 134

Baked Ham With Mustard Glaze 87

Baked Vegetables 102

Bananas; 90

Banana Cream Pie 90

Basil; 94, 142

Beans; 16, 44, 89, 94, 102, 112, 142

BEANS:
  Baby Lima Beans 44
  Green Beans, Fresh 89
  Green Beans with Pears and Bacon 16

BEEF:
  Brisket 54
  Meatballs, *Konisberger Klopse* 12
  Meat Tarts, *Sfihas* 39
  Rita's Burritos 112
  Roast Beef with Vegetables 58
  Tamale Pie, with ground beef 125

Black Eyed Peas 134

BREADS:
  Buttermilk Biscuits 47
  Lemon Bread 113
  Yorkshire Pudding 59

Brisket 54

Broccoli; 94, 102, 108, 118

Broccoli, Cheese and Rice Casserole 118

Browned Butter Banana Cream Pie 90

Brunch Eggs 68

Brussels Sprouts; 29

Burritos 112

Butter & Cheese Noodles 28

Buttermilk Biscuits 47

C

Cajun Greens 131

CAKE:
  1234 Cake 126
  Alma's Italian Cream Cake 32
  Lemon Bread 113
  Lemon Cake 74

CHEESE:
  Cheese Kugel 53
  Knishes, Audrey's Famous Cheese 52

Capers; 12, 29

Carrots; 58, 72, 94, *102, 108, 142, 147*

Cat's Brussels Sprouts 29

Cauliflower, fried 38

Cauliflower; 38, 102, 108

Cheese; 26, 30, 52, 53, 140

Cheese Knishes 52

Cheese Kugel 53

Chervil; 140

Chicken; 26, 72, 81, 98, 102, 116, 124, 130, 139, 147

Chicken and Dressing 116

Chicken and Dumplin's 124